WOLVES

WOLVES
A Wildlife Handbook

Kim Long

SCIENTIFIC ADVISOR
Dr. Randall Lockwood, Ph.D.

Johnson Books
BOULDER

Published in the United States by Johnson Books, a Division of Johnson Publishing Company, 1880 South 57th Court, Boulder, Colorado 80301.

9 8 7 6 5 4 3 2 1

Cover design: Margaret Donharl
Cover illustration: Kim Long
All illustrations by the author unless otherwise indicated.

Library of Congress Cataloging-in-Publication Data
Long, Kim.
    Wolves: a wildlife handbook / Kim Long.
        p. cm.
    Includes bibliographical references (p.   ) and index.
    ISBN 1-55566-158-0 (alk. paper)
    1. Wolves.   I. Title
QL737.C22L65   1996
599.74'442 — dc20   96-26553
                                                CIP

Printed in the United States by
Johnson Printing
1880 South 57th Court
Boulder, Colorado 80301

 Printed on recycled paper with soy ink

CONTENTS

ACKNOWLEDGMENTS

Dr. Randall Lockwood, Humane Society of the U.S.
Dr. James Halfpenny
Gregory McNamee
Michael McNierney
Bill Higginson
The Bloomsbury Review
Denver Public Library
Western History Collection, Denver Public Library
Norlin Library, University of Colorado
Auraria Library, Metropolitan State College
Stage House II Books, Boulder, Colorado
Kathleen Cain, Front Range Community College

INTRODUCTION

Wolves would be experiencing a renaissance in popularity in our modern era, except that they were never very popular to begin with. The birth of what we consider civilization was a consequence of the development of agriculture and the establishment of domesticated animals as a source of meat, milk, beasts of burden, and clothing. Before these tame creatures came along, wolves most likely had little to do with humans; after, it was a different story.

As long as herds of animals have existed, wolves have been a bane to human cultures — chased, hunted, reviled, and feared for their predation. Because of their hunting prowess, intelligence, and strength, they have also generated superstition, myth, and deification. But unlike other powerful animals — the bear, lion, or eagle, for example — the constant depredations against livestock generated more negative feelings than positive. The sight of wolves scavenging the bodies of dead humans magnified their threat, if only in the imagination. This has been the story since the earliest known civilizations in Europe and Asia. In North America, domesticated animals — except for dogs — were missing until the arrival of European settlers and the two cultures — wolf and human — remained farther apart. The wolf's image was therefore more dignified and positive among native cultures on the continent. The arrival of European explorers and settlers, along with horses, cows, pigs, and sheep, altered this natural balance.

In the tradition of animal mythology among the original North American cultures, coyotes have had a stronger and broader role. Often, coyotes win contests of skill and cleverness when pitted against wolves. This may seem incongruous in light of our current knowledge about wolves, but may make sense in the perspective of ancient balances of nature. Before European settlers arrived and radically changed the ecology of North America, coyotes were relatively scarce compared to wolves, and their natural range was much smaller than it is today. To native Americans, the wolf may have been common and the coyote rare, a situation that may have imparted more mystery and power to the coyote. As the wolf was removed from its native range — most of the continent — the coyote population expanded to take its place. Now, the coyote appears to us as common and the wolf rare. The coyote in modern North American eyes is often a pest and the rarely seen wolf is the top dog in the pantheon of power among wildlife.

THE BEASTLY STORY

"O a shadowy beast is the gaunt gray wolf!
And his feet fall soft on a carpet of spines;
Where the night shuts quick and the winds are cold
He haunts the deeps of the northern pines."

— Hamlin Garland, 1899

In human history, wolves have had a checkered reputation. Reviled for their ravenous appetites and ferocious manner, they were also admired for their strength, intelligence, and loyalty. Competing with humans for food, they have made an indelible impression among the human cultures in their range.

The story of wolves has had a different slant in North America than in Europe and Asia. In the New World, native cultures had no livestock until the arrival of European settlers and had little interaction with wolves. In the "Old World," on the other hand, expanding populations of people, the development of agriculture, the development of domesticated animals, and urban sprawl had an earlier and more profound impact on how wolves fared in the human imagination. And at the same time, some biologists believe that wolves in Asia and Europe evolved with different physiology and behaviors than their counterparts in North America. But wherever wolves existed, they evoked similar responses from human cultures. The wolf was always identified as a predator and devourer of flesh, an enemy of people and their livestock. In the *Bible*, wolves are described as devouring creatures, tamed only by the hand of God. In the *Koran*, the wolf is feared for its capability to devour humans. Even earlier in recorded history, Artistotle, about 350 B.C., described some animals as "... thorough-bred and wild and treacherous, as the wolf."

Just as in the New World, however, wolves were originally most likely to have kept their distance from human habitations, finding adequate territory and prey in which to thrive apart from people.

THE LANGUAGE OF WOLVES

ACHUMAWI	chemoo	FRENCH	loup
AINU	horkeu	GAULISH	succellus
ALBANIAN	ujk	GERMAN	wolf
ALGONQUIAN	tuk'sit	GOTHIC	vargr
APACHE	mah'cho	GREEK	loukhos
ARABIC	tha'lab	HITTITE	ulippanna
ARMENIAN	gail	HOPI	kweeuu
BASQUE	otso	HUNGARIAN	farkas
BENGALI	shial	INUKTITUT	singarti
BRETON	bleiz	IÑUPIAT	amaguk
BULGARIAN	vulk	IRISH	cu allaidh
BYELORUSSIAN	vowk	ISLETA	k'y'jo
CADDO	tasho	ITALIAN	lupo
CAHUILLA	iswet	JAPANESE	ohkami
CATALAN	llop	KIOWA	mokuyi
CHEROKEE	wahy'a	KOREAN	nukde
CHEYENNE	maiyun	KOYUKON	teekkona
CHINESE	lang	KWAKIUTL	gwala
CHIPEWYAN	segolia	LAKOTA	suuk manitu tanka
CHIPPEWA	gun'iew	LATIN	lupus
CREE	maheegan	LATVIAN	vilks
CROATIAN	vuk	LENAPE	mohegan
CZECH	vluku	LITHUANIAN	vilkas
DANISH	ulf	LUSHOOTSEED	štiqáyu'
DUTCH	wolf	MANDARIN CHINESE	lang
ESKIMO	oo koo'a	MENOMINI	moquiao
ETRUSCAN	oltas	MONGOLIAN	yeono
FINNISH	susi	NAVAJO	ma'iitsoh

NOOTKA	*lokwa'*	SLOVENIAN	*volk*
OLD ENGLISH	*wulf*	SPANISH	*lobo*
PAWNEE	*skiri'ki*	SWAHILI	*mbwa mwitu*
PERSIAN	*walkuwa*	SWEDISH	*varg*
POLISH	*wilk*	TEWA	*ko'yo*
PORTUGUESE	*lobo*	TIBETAN	*cungqu*
ROMANIAN	*lup*	TOCHARIAN	*walkwe*
RUSSIAN	*volk*	TOHONO O'ODHAM	*sheh'e*
SAMNITE	*hirpus*	TURKISH	*kurt*
SANSKRIT	*vrka*	UTE	*sunawavi*
SENECA	*kyiyu*	VIETNAMESE	*con chó sói*
SERRANO	*wanat*	YAQUI	*hunama wo'i*
SHOSHONE	*beya ish*	YIDDISH	*volf*

List entries compiled by Greg McNamee

WOLF WORDS

The English word "wolf" comes from an Old English word, "wulf." In ancient forms of the Norse language, it was "ulfr." Anglo-Saxons in ancient England called the month of January "wulf-monath," noting the time of year when wolves were most likely to be on the prowl for food. A few hundred years ago, the word was also adopted to mean an older male who preyed upon younger men.

MORE WOLF WORDS

Other English words that have adopted "wolf" include ...

wolfberry (the mountain cranberry)
wolf herring (a fish from tropical areas of the Pacific)
wolf teeth (curved teeth on gears used in some watches)
wolfsbane (an herb native to Eurasia)
wolf's milk (spurge, a plant with a milky juice)
wolf's moss (Letharia vulpina, an alpine lichen)
wolf snake (a snake native to southeastern Asia)
wolf's peach (an archaic term for tomato)
wolf spider (a variety of spider in the Lycosidae family)
wolf tree
wolf whistle
wolf willow (buffalo berry)
wolfram, wolframite (one of the first names for tungsten)
wolf pack
wolf grape (chicken grape)
wolf eel (a fish from the Pacific Coast of North America)
sea-wolf (same as wolf-fish)
river-wolf
aard-wolf
tiger-wolf
wolf moth
wolf's fist (a type of puffball)
wolf net
wolf fly
Wolfland (formerly used as a name for Ireland)
wolfstone (also dogstone)
wolf thistle
wolf tick
wolf willow
lupus, the disease, was originally referred to as the Wolfe

The development of permanent human settlements was the key factor in altering this natural balance. Agriculture — requiring the clearing of lands for fields and pastures — and fuel — requiring the clearing of forests for firewood — simultaneously removed natural habitat and provided an abundant supply of new and easy-to-kill prey.

Beginning in the Middle Ages, widespread war, famines, and epi-

Illustration titled "European Bison, Attacked by Wolves," from *Buffon's Natural History of Man, the Globe, and of Quadrapeds* (1879, Hurst & Company, New York City).

Heraldry is a system of traditional designs and symbols used to denote family identity in England and Europe. The image of the wolf appears in the crests for many families with this heritage, including Fuller, Miller, Seale, Sutton, Lowe, and Wilson.

"The Woolves be in some respect different from them in other countries; it was never knowne yet that a Woolfe ever set upon a man or a woman."
— William A. Wood
New England's Prospect, 1635

demics offered wolves increasing opportunities for interaction with people. For the first time within the wolves' natural range, large concentrations of meat — dead people — created new sources of food for this opportunistic hunter. At the same time that populations were expanding into the traditional hunting territory of the wolf, the populations themselves could have provided prime scavenging potential. Especially during the long-lasting and brutal wars that charcterized long periods of Asian and European history, wolves may have lost some of their traditional shyness toward humans.

Although the wolf must have been recognized as a serious preda-

WOLF SITES

In North America, many towns and geographical features have been named after the wolf. Including variations such as "wolfden," "wolfpit," "wolf run," "wolf fang," and "wolf head," there are more than 2,400 such listings in the United States alone. The coyote, in comparison, has only 956 listings.

towns	68	ridges	45
parks	36	flats	18
gaps and passes	47	lakes	139
summits	160	cliffs	7
swamps	35	capes	19
valleys	184	caves	13
springs	29	streams	1019

tor even in prehistoric times, it may not have been until wolves and people edged closer together that negative images of wolves first emerged. Along the way, the dog was domesticated from a wolf ancestry and became a frequent and valued member of human communities. Where dogs were valued for their subservience, loyalty, and protection, they also offered a constant perspective to the wolf, whose similar appearance represented none of the dogs' valued attributes. The very characteristics that made the dog appreciated may have worked against the wolf, a dog-like animal that attacked and devoured instead of serving its masters.

The already-negative image of the wolf deteriorated even further as the animal developed a reputation as a scavenger of dead bodies.

"[The wolf] is one of those animals whose appetite for animal food is the most vehement, and whose means of satisfying this appetite are the most various. Nature has furnished him with strength, with cunning, with agility, with all those requisite, in a word, which fit an animal for pursuing, overtaking, and conquering its prey; and yet, with all these, the Wolf most frequently dies of hunger; for he is the declared enemy of man."

"The Wolf, as well externally as internally, so nearly resembles the dog, that he seems modelled upon the same plan; and yet he only offers the reverse of the image. If his form be similar, his nature is different; and indeed they are so unlike in their dispositions, that no two animals can have a more perfect antipathy to each other."

— Georges Louis Leclerc Buffon
Buffon's Natural History of Man, the Globe, and of Quadrapeds, 1879

"Mr. John D. Wilcox, of Pine City, Superintendent of Schools for Pine county, told me that about the year 1860, when he lived at Sunrise in Chicago county, having worked through a winter day in the woods, making sugar-troughs, one and a half miles from home, which was at Sunrise, he was chased by a half dozen or more wolves, which he saw bounding up and down in their pursuit on his track, and heard their yelping; with the greatest haste possible he got across the open land where he then was and climbed up into a tree, but only barely in time to save himself, for the wolves were immediately at the tree, jumping up, yelping, and making the evening hideous. This continued two hours or more, the wolves all the time howling and leaping up, their eyes glowing like coals of fire. Finally they got into a fight among themselves and turned off into a neighboring swamp. This fight with much crashing of the alders, snarling and yelping of the wolves, and joy of Mr. W., to hear his foes waging war on each other, lasted an hour or so; then all became as still as death, he finally got down and escaped home. His axe, left at the foot of the tree, had its handle so gnawed and split that it was spoiled. Woodsmen have a saying that when a pack of wolves thus are foiled and lose their expected prey, they turn on the wolf that first led them into the pursuit and slay him."

— C. L. Herrick
Mammals of Minnesota: A Scientific and Popular Account of Their Features and Habits, 1892

Anyone witnessing this predator feeding on a human body might be expected to have ugly thoughts, especially since it so closely resembled "man's best friend," the dog. But the most serious problem for the wolf has always been the expanding encroachment of its native turf for human agricultural purposes. Cleared land used for crops diminishes the grazing habitats required by the wolves' traditional prey, and the increasing use of domesticated animals, particularly sheep, pigs, and cattle, has replaced many herds of wild animals. Wolves altered their own hunting behavior in response to this change, becoming a serious threat for settlements that depended on their animals for food, clothing, and economic power. As early as Roman times, official government policies have included bounties on wolves and even taxes required to be paid in wolf hides. The civ-

WOLF NICKNAMES

Israel Putnam, an American military commander during the Revolution, was nicknamed "Wolf" Putnam. Born in Massachusetts in 1718, Putnam gained his nickname during the pursuit of a wolf which had raided and killed many sheep. In a biography published in 1818, it was reported that the renegade animal was a "she wolf" which "had for several years infested the vicinity." After tracking the wolf to its lair in a cave, Putnam crawled into the cave with a torch and a rifle and shot the animal at close quarters. Another noted American with the "Wolf" nickname was Ernest Thompson Seton. Born in 1860, Seton acquired his nickname as a famous wolf hunter. Seton also helped promote the concept of conservation by writing about the natural history of wild animals in the United States. Animal names were widely used among North American Indians, including many variations based on the wolf.

ilized world in Europe and Asia operated in direct opposition to the
wolves' natural habits. As civilization spread, so too did this confrontation.

Wolves virtually disappeared from England by 1500 and were
probably extinct there soon after the turn of that century, killed off
by the relentless pressure against them. In Ireland and Scotland,
the native wolves were exterminated by the late 1700s. Wolves on
the European continent were gone from most areas except the most
mountainous by the end of the 1800s; most parts of the continent
were wolf-free at least one hundred years earlier. In the twentieth
century, wolves exist in Europe in small numbers in Spain and
Portugal, an isolated park in Italy, Czechoslovakia, Poland, and
parts of Scandinavia. Wolf populations exist in healthy numbers
only in Siberia. Fewer than 1,000 wolves are thought to survive in
India and scattered populations exist in parts of southwestern and
south-central Asia.

The New World civilizations had much different experiences and

Illustration by Bert R. Elliott for "The Three Little Pigs," from *The Child's
Treasury* (1923, Foundation Desk Company, Chicago).

reactions to wolves. Native American cultures generally promoted the image of the wolf as a powerful and able hunter, although it was occasionally hunted itself for its fur and meat. The rapid spread of horses through western Indian cultures may, however, have altered this balance, as wolves preyed upon these domesticated animals when convenient.

Both Old and New World records of human-wolf encounters and the legends that were found in most cultures could have been influenced by one untypical form of wolf behavior. Wolves — as well as other mammals — that are afflicted with rabies can lose their natural shyness and become aggressive and unpredictable. Some or all of the cases of wolves attacking humans in Europe, Asia, and North America may be attributed to this disease. In those cases of wolf attacks where the wolves have been observed, studied, or tested, rabies is almost always present. At least based on recent history in North America, healthy wolves have consistently maintained a careful distance from people and urban locations. Although there are many stories of wolves attacking and killing humans, no one has yet been able to prove that this has happened on this continent.

Wolves became potent symbols for evil in Europe, attacked for their actual destruction of livestock and imagined connection to satanic forces. Human outlaws were often referred to as wolves. In the Roman empire, a person convicted of matricide had his head covered by a wolfskin. During the Middle Ages, wolves were sometimes hanged on the gallows beside human criminals. In the long-running battle between civilization and wolves, the wolves lost their reputation as well as their lives.

WOLVES IN
THE AMERICAS

"There is a strong feeling of hostility entertained by the settlers of the wild portions of the country, toward the Wolf, as his strength, agility, and cunning, (in which last qualification, he is scarcely inferior to his relative, the fox,) tend to render him the most destructive enemy of their pigs, sheep, or young calves, which range in the forest; therefore, in our country, he is not more mercifully dealt with than in any other part of the world."
— John James Audubon, Rev. John Bachman, 1851

Tribal cultures in North America coexisted with wolves for generations without serious problems. Most likely because people on this continent had little in the way of domesticated livestock — dogs were the most widespread — the wolves here rarely had a direct impact on local peoples.

The more or less balanced coexistence between people and wolves here began to change shortly after the arrival of the first European explorers and settlers. In the East, it was the introduction of domesticated animals such as pigs, sheep, and cattle that began to shift the natural balance. These creatures — along with the already present population of wild game that was considered essential for survival — first began to pit the wolf against the needs of the new civilization.

In the West, it was the arrival and rapid spread of the horse that upset the existing order. Horses, at least after they were adopted by western tribes, altered traditional lifestyles and the hunting methods used to reap the most bountiful source of meat throughout the west, the buffalo. Mostly stalked and hunted singly before the horse, slain buffalo were used frugally and completely, leaving little

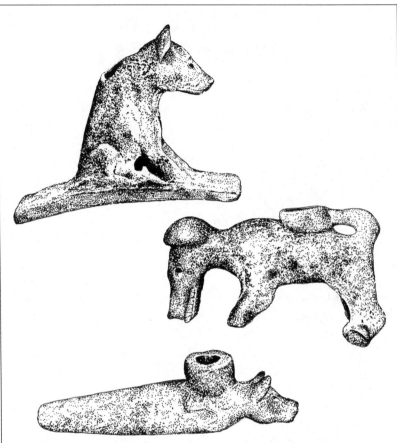

Wolf effigy pipes from a collection in the Ohio State Museum. These pipes were found in the Tremper Mound, situated near the present city of Portsmouth, Ohio. The mound was constructed by a tribe of the Hopewell culture, a pre-Columbian culture that thrived from approximately 500 B.C. to about 500 A.D. These pipes were made of pipestone (catlinite), a soft mineralized clay found in southwestern Minnesota and widely traded throughout the midwestern and eastern native American populations. Size: each is about 3.5 x 2.5 inches (90 mm x 60 mm).

ORIGINAL RANGE OF THE BISON

The original range of the bison covered most of the continent. By the 1880s, this territory had shrunk by more than half; by the end of the 1800s, bison were found only in Wyoming, Montana, and the Dakotas.

"It is said that when visiting battle-fields in Mexico, the Wolves preferred the slain Texans or Americans, to the Mexicans, and only ate the bodies of the latter from necessity, as owing to the quantity of pepper used by the Mexicans in their food, their flesh is impregnated with that powerful stimulant. Not vouching for this story, however, the fact is well known that these animals follow the movements of armies, or at least are always at hand to prey upon the slain before their comrades can give them a soldier's burial, or even after that mournful rite; and if anything could increase the horrors displayed by the gory ensanguined field, where man has slain his fellows by thousands, it would be the presence of packs of these ravenous beasts disputing for the carcasses of the brave, the young, and the patriotic, who have fallen for their country's honour!"

— John James Audubon, Rev. John Bachman
The Quadrupeds of North America, 1851

edible material for wolves to scavenge. After the arrival of the horse, tribes expanded rapidly because of their new efficiency at food gathering. Although Native Americans were still conservative in how many buffalo they killed and how much of each buffalo was utilized for food and clothing, there was an increasing number of carcasses scattered across the western regions throughout the seasons, a potent catalyst that prompted the rapid expansion of the wolf population.

A culture with one of the closest connections to wolves was the Pawnee tribe. The Pawnees thought of themselves as skilled warriors who shared many of attributes of the wolf. They endured long periods of travel, scavenged food from carcasses or went long periods without eating, and were capable of stealthily avoiding detection by their enemies. Pawnees were also known to use wolf skins to disguise themselves as the real animal, sneaking close to buffalo herds or into enemy encampments to steal horses.

The arrival of fur traders, miners, ranchers, farmers, and other settlers from the East in the early 1800s marked the beginning of an unprecedented era of feasting for the plains wolf. By the time widespread buffalo hunting had become a trend, packs of wolves were a constant presence throughout the buffalo's range. Buffalo hunting became an organized and efficient operation, so thorough and voracious in its appetite for animals that between 1870 and 1880, an estimated 20 million buffalo were killed. Not just in numbers, however, but in unused meat, the buffalo remains left behind these operations provided a limitless supply of food for the wolf population.

The arrival of the first railroads in the western territories was also instrumental in the widescale hunting of buffalo and their subsequent demise. In 1866, the first cattle drive from Texas to Kansas was held to bring livestock to the newly-arrived railroad. Between 1866 and 1883, an estimated 4.7 million head of cattle were part of

"The wolfes are of divers coloures: some sandy coloured; some griselled, and some black, their foode is fish which they catch when they passe up the rivers, into the ponds to spawne, at the spring time...They are fearefull Curres, and will runne away from a man (that meeteth them by chance at a banke end) as fast as any feareful dogge. These pray upon the Deare very much."

— Thomas Morton
New English Canaan or New Canaan, 1637, Amsterdam

July 18. ... We have passt some 12 graves & I am told there is a burying ground near here of 300 graves ... I see some painfull sights where the wolves have taken up the dead & torn their garments in pieces & in some instances the skulls & jaw bones are strewed over the ground.

August 26. Started early, went 19 miles ... Crosst Sage creek & on the bank saw the grave of a young man dug up & his body nearly eat up by wolves.

— Lucena Parsons (from diary kept during trip from Wisconsin to California in 1850)

Saturday 25th May 1822, the Wolves maid an atackt on our Horse the[y] Wounded one Hors and two mules We Havbe maid a strong Pen Close to the Camp and Still Shut up all the Horses at night While We Remain at this Place to protect them for the Wolfes.

— Elliott Coues, ed. *The Journal of Jacob Fowler,* 1898

this herding activity. Beginning in the 1870s, western cattlemen began publicly complaining about losses to wolves. At about this time, associations were first formed to provide cattlemen with political influence, negotiations with railroads, and dealing with rustling and natural predators. Although the western territories had already by this time established bounties on wolves, the cattle organizations offered additional rewards for wolves destroyed and also supplied regular supplies of poison — mostly strychnine — for range riders to use on all available carcasses, including buffalo and livestock.

With the sudden and almost complete destruction of the buffalo herds — the last large herds in the northern region were gone by 1884 — the newly-expanded population of wolves was left without its regular diet and an inevitable confrontation began, between these predators and the herds of cattle and sheep that settlers had brought with them to the West. With cattle and sheep lost in large numbers, wolves were targeted and systematically eradicated to provide safe pasturage and rangeland for the newcomers. In only a few decades, once numerous sightings of wolves were reduced to reports of occasional regional marauders, so few that most were stigmatized with individual names.

By the early 1900s, the last wolves had disappeared in most of the west. In 1924, the last wolf was spotted in California; in 1974, the last wolf disappeared from Oregon.

THE WOLF MYTH

"It is reported that there are wolves in Italy, who when they looke upon a man, cause him to be silent that hee cannot speake." — Edward Topsell, 1607

Few animals have as strong a symbolic presence in human cultures as does the wolf. Because of this animal's widespread natural range — throughout Asia, Europe, and the Americas — and formidable activity as a predator, the wolf has long been the object of myth and superstition.

In the sky, the constellation Lupus represents the wolf. Named by the Greeks, Lupus lies close to the horizon and is bordered by Centaurus, Circinus, Libra, Norma, and Scorpius. In the year 1006, a supernova, the explosion of a star, was observed in this constellation in Europe and in parts of the Arabian empire, the first and only such stellar activity to be recorded before the Renaissance. Lupus is one of the oldest named constellations, one of forty-eight original Greek stellar bodies. Centaurus, a neighboring constellation, may have originally been portrayed in the act of spearing Lupus as a sacrificial offering.

In North America, Blackfoot Indian origin myths describe stellar beings Sun, Moon, and Morning Star who live in Sky-country. In their mythology, the Milky Way is called the Wolf-trail. Pawnees also shared this image of the Milky Way; they referred to it as the Wolf Road. A folktale of the Pawnee tells of Wolf, who lived with people and shared their meat until Paruksti, the Western Storm, convinced them to kill him. The gods were angry at this reaction and bade the people call themselves Skidi, Wolf-People, and those that had done the deed were turned into wolves themselves. The spirit of Wolf was made holy and ascended to the sky as Tskirixki-tiuhats, Star of Deceiver Wolf, rising in the east before the morning star. Waiting for the appearance of the morning star to begin

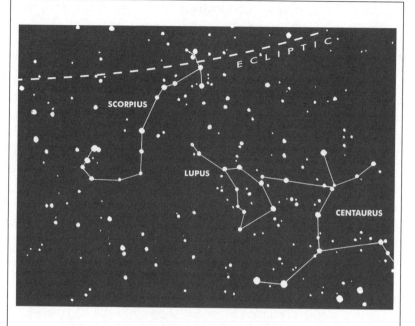

LUPUS, THE WOLF

Between Scorpio and Centaurus lies the
constellation of Lupus, the Wolf. Not every
culture has interpreted this star pattern as a
wolf, however. Originally, the Greeks and
Romans designated this pattern as the Beast, or
Wild Animal. Some early Arabs called it the
Lioness, and others combined it with the stars of
Centaurus and called it the Palm Branches. In
1006 A.D., a supernova appeared within this
constellation, near the star Beta Lupi. Observed
and chronicled in medieval records in Europe,
Egypt, and Asia, this was the earliest known
observation of the birth of a star.

howling, the people-turned-wolves on earth are themselves deceived, and howl in greeting.

The city/state of Rome, founded in 753 B.C., is traditionally linked to the legend of Romulus and Remus. The twins were born to Mars, the god of war, through an illicit liaison with Rhea Silvia, a vestal virgin. As punishment for her transgression, they were set adrift on the Tiber River, abandoned to a certain death from starvation. According to the legend, a she-wolf adopted the pair and suckled them as if they were her own offspring. During the Roman empire, an annual festival was held to honor the wolf. The festival of the Lupercalia was held on the site where the twins were supposedly found, a cave on Palatine Hill. Priests known as Luperci sacrificed goats and dogs during this festival. The Latin word for wolf, lupa, however, also means prostitute, allowing for an entirely different interpretation of this myth.

In Greek mythology, Zeus (a.k.a. Jupiter), disguised as an ordinary traveler, left the heavens and made a visit to the palace of King Lycaon. There, he revealed himself as a god, but the King was not convinced of his true identity. As a cruel test, he murdered Arcas, the son of Zeus by his wife Callisto, and prepared a meal for Zeus from the body of the dead boy. When served this diabolical dish, Zeus was outraged and threw a thunderbolt at King Lycaon, turning him into a wolf. Other traditional Greek symbology linked the moon divinity to a female wolf.

The Greek sun-god Apollo was born to Leto, known as a she-wolf. Apollo had human wives and sent wolves to suckle the children of these unions. Apollo himself was sometimes known as a wolf-god and could take the form of a wolf when necessary. Human worship of Apollo in the Greek empire involved wolves, which were either sacrificed or received sacrifices of meat.

The origin myth of Turkey tells of its founder being suckled by a she-wolf. Early Turks sometimes referred to themselves as "Sons of the Wolf." Ancient Yugoslavian mythology dating to the thirteenth

"The Law of the Jungle lays down very clearly that any wolf may, when he marries, withdraw from the Pack he belongs to; but as soon as his cubs are old enough to stand on their feet he must bring them to the Pack council, which is generally held once a month at full moon, in order that the other wolves may identify them. After that inspection the cubs are free to run where they please, and until they have killed their first buck no excuse is accepted if a grown wolf of the Pack kills one of them. The punishment is death where the murderer can be found; and if you think for a minute you will see that this must be so.

Father Wolf waited till his cubs could run a little, and then on the night of the Pack Meeting took them and Mowgli and Mother Wolf to the Council Rock — a hilltop covered with stones and boulders where a hundred wolves could hide. Akela, the great gray Lone Wolf, who led all the Pack by strength and cunning, lay out at full length on his rock, and below him sat forty or more wolves of every size and colour, from badger-coloured veterans who could handle a buck alone, to young black three-year-olds who thought they could. The Lone Wolf had led them for a year now. He had fallen twice into a wolf trap in his youth, and once he had been beaten and left for dead; so he knew the manners and customs of men. There was very little talking at the Rock. The cubs tumbled over each other in the centre of the circle where their mothers and father sat, and now and again a senior wolf would go quietly up to a cub, look at him carefully, and return to his place on noiseless feet. Sometimes a mother would push her cub far out into the moonlight, to be sure that he had not been overlooked. Akela from his rock would cry: "Ye know the Law — ye know the Law. Look well, O Wolves!" and the anxious mothers would take up the call: "Look — look well, O Wolves!"

— Rudyard Kipling
The Jungle Books, 1895

century describes Vukodlak, a werewolf being who ate the moon, a primitive explanation of a lunar eclipse. Wolves were usually portrayed as villainous beasts in myths from Hindu cultures. The Celtic gods included Lok, who was in the form of a wolf. Lok symbolized destructive power.

Some ancient Egyptians belonged to a sect of wolf-worshippers. Associated with the city of Lycopolis, these people followed rituals that replicated the eating habits of wolves in the wild. In one ancient Egyptian legend, Ap-uat is a wolf-god who plays a part in the after-life.

Traditional Scandinavian myths tell of Fenrir, a wolf god who was the offspring of Loki. A large and dangerous being, Fenrir was devoted to Tyr, the god of war, who provided him with food. Large and threatening, Fenrir's power worried the other gods, and they plotted to constrain him with a harness made from the powers of earth. Tyr was chosen to place the harness on Fenrir, but lost his

Illustration of European "black wolf" from the early 1800s.

hand in the process. Another Scandinavian myth is about Managram, a wolf who laps up the blood of the dead, infuses the sky with blood, and devours the moon. In the classic Norse epic *Edda,* wolves are prominent figures. The wolves Sköll and Hati target the sun and the moon as sources of food. In the saga, a witch rides a wolf with bridles formed by eagles and one wolf becomes a eunuch; wolves also compete against humans for treasure.

Some Christian mythology also involves wolves, possibly connected to actual historical events. In one such tale, a pack of wolves in 617 A.D. attacked a monastery and killed several friars who held heretical beliefs.

Another such legend holds that God himself sent wolves to protect

"Black wolf" from an 18th century book illustration.

the sacking of the holy house of Loreto by the Duke of Urbino. Wolves were said to have guarded the severed head of St. Edmund the Martyr. The Abbot of Cluny, St. Oddo, was attacked by foxes while on a pilgrimage, but a wolf saved him. One Christian myth about Saint Francis involves a wolf. In the town of Gubbino, a ravenous wolf was terrorizing the local populace. Saint Francis, deliberately seeking out this beast, tamed him with the sign of the cross.

Ancient Indian fables include one about a wolf. In this tale, an archer, after killing a deer, was gored by a charging boar after it was shot with an arrow. The three dead bodies were discovered by a passing wolf who was confounded by his luck. Determining to hoard this bounty for later meals, he decided to eat only the smallest, most insignificant part of the cache. Biting on the gut string of the archer's bow, it snapped, whipping the bow across his throat in a fatal slash.

Myths about wolves often represent religious themes, concepts that helped to explain unknown forces. As literature developed as a form of entertainment, however, many myths evolved into less powerful forms such as folktales. Jacob and Wilhelm Grimm, German brothers who were born in the late 1700s, created some of the best known folktales. Among them are several involving wolves. "The Wolf and the Seven Kids" is one of these, presenting the dark cliché of the wolf as a horrid, wicked beast. In this story, the ravenous wolf talks his way into the home of the mother goat while she is away. One by one, he swallows six of the seven kids whole, but the seventh one hides inside a grandfather clock. Upon returning home, the horrified mother goat hears the news from the surviving kid. While walking through their garden, however, they come across the wolf, sleeping off his heavy meal. The mother goat slits open the wolf's stomach and rescues all of her offspring alive, as they have been swallowed whole. Replacing each kid with a stone, she sews up the wolf's stomach. Upon waking, the wolf goes to the local river to drink, where the weight of the stones tips him into the water to drown. This tale, in a few variations, was also known in Slavic and Russian cultures.

NATIVE AMERICAN MYTHS

*"Ah, they are wise, true-hearted animals,
the big wolves of the plains."* — Red Eagle

In Iroquois mythology, the origin of their tribe and the earth was linked to six men who existed at the beginning. One of the men, named Hoguaho (Wolf), was sent to heaven to find a woman who was thought to live there. Seduced with a gift of bear fat, she was cast out by the master of heavens and landed on the back of a turtle, where an island was formed to receive her. She bore two children, from whom all men were descended; the subsequent descendants were divided into three families linked to the three original animal entities, the bear, the turtle, and the wolf.

In the Menomini creation myth, twin brothers are responsible for naming all the animals of the world. One of the twins is the wolf, who also supplies his brother with food from his hunts. One day, while swimming across a lake inhabited by evil beings, the wolf is drowned. The twin brother, in mourning, caused hills and valleys to form. The Chippewas of Wisconsin have an origin myth in which the hero's guardian spirit is a wolf. In Chippewa myths, wolves provide humans with food and hides. Nez Perce creation stories also credit wolves as being the origin of the human race. A traditional tale from the Eskimos of Cape Prince of Wales is about a young woman who marries a stranger and endures several mysterious adventures among his people. After a long life together, they both turn into wolves.

The Zuni believe that the wolf spirit represents the east, one of the six cardinal directions (North, South, East, West, Up, and Below). The wolf is the chief of the hunt, and prayers and offerings made to him will insure his assistance during the search for

Sign language for "Pawnee"
or "wolf"

(redrawn from *Pawnee Hero Stories
and Folk-Tales*, by George Bird
Grinnell, 1889)

Native American cultures in the western regions of North America shared a common language of hand signs. Using this sign language, one way to make the "wolf" word was as follows: the right hand held with palm out, the first and second fingers extended in a "V" pointing upward while the other fingers and thumb were closed together. The hand is then moved several inches up and forward. The sign for "coyote" was the same as for wolf, adding a sign for "small." In some tribes, the signs were the same for "wolf" and "dog," with the dog sign the same as the above, but upside down as the hand is moved parallel to the body. This symbolizes the traditional role of the dog in some tribes, a carrier of teepee or lodge poles (travois). A variation on this sign was used to denote the Pawnees, a tribe symbolized by the wolf. The right hand was held close to the shoulder, palm forward with the first two fingers in a "V" pointing upward while the other fingers and thumb were closed. The hand was then bent at the wrist, the pointing fingers moving forward. The fingers thus represented the upright ears of a wolf.

game. The Nootka Wolf Dance is another ritual offering to a wolf spirit, reenacting the ancestors' visit to the House of Wolves.

The Cree Indian creation myth tells of a wolf who forms the first land. Flooded by a broken beaver dam, the earth was covered with water. The hero, Wisagatcak, turned to the wolf for help and the wolf ran in circles around a floating raft with a clump of moss in his mouth. As he ran, the moss grew, covering the raft and forming the earth.

One traditional myth of the Senecas tells of a war chief known as Ganogwioeo who was captured during a war raid against a Cherokee village. Ganogwioeo escaped while being tortured and began a long trek through the wilderness without food, clothing, or shelter. During this escape, two mysterious men came to him each night and provided him with meat, clothing, and warmth. When he finally neared safety, he turned to say goodbye to his benefactors and saw them turn into wolves, one white and one black.

In the traditional Lakota Sioux belief system, Sungmanitu, the Spirit of the Wolf, accompanied individuals during war parties or when chasing after a prey animal. Woziya, the North Wind, is identified with the white owl, the raven and the wolf. These animals are his aides (tonweyapi), functioning as soldiers, spies, and counselors as the situation dictates. In general, the Sioux considered the wolves as wakan, or entities with supernatural power. The wolf thus has special meaning in a variety of contexts and was a positive symbol. In a dream, for instance, the image of the wolf signified stealthiness, the ability to approach enemies without being detected. If a gun is used to shoot a wolf, the gun will be rendered useless. At times, however, the wolf may symbolize negativity. If a person hears a wolf howl, for instance, it may signify that something will go wrong.

Delaware Indians thought that a change of weather might be brought on by the howling of a wolf. They also believed that a wolf's bark would bestow long life upon a person. Traditional Kwakiutl Indian lore states that a bow or gun used to kill a wolf is unlucky and must be given away. In the Coast Salish tribe, if a wolf was shot, it was feared that other wolves would surround the hunter and kill him unless he apologized for his misdeed.

"All the wolves in Hudson's Bay are very shy of the human race, yet when sharp set, they frequently follow the Indians for several days, but always keep a distance. They are great enemies to the Indian dogs, and frequently kill and eat those that are heavy loaded, and cannot keep up with the main body. The Northern Indians have formed strange ideas of the animal, as they think it does not eat its victuals raw; but by a singular and wonderful sagacity, peculiar to itself, has a method of cooling them without fire."

— Samuel Hearne, 1772

WEREWOLVES

"Wolf-madness, is a disease, in which men run barking and howling about graves and fields in the night, lying hid for the most part all day, and will not be persuaded but that they are Wolves, or some such beasts."

— Robert Bayfield, 1663

One of the longest-lasting themes in folklore is human beings who are transformed into wolves. As far back as the ancient Greeks, tales have been told of people turned into wolves, often as a consequence of their beliefs or actions. The King Lycaon, for instance, was transformed by Zeus into a wolf as a punishment for murdering Zeus's son and serving him to Zeus at a meal. A shrine to Zeus at Mount Lycaeus was said to be used for human sacrifices and worshippers who feasted on the bodies of the victims were then turned into wolves.

Zeus was celebrated in the ancient Greek era with a festival held every nine years. During the rituals held for this festival, a boy would be killed as a sacrifice to Zeus and his intestines made into a soup along with those from sheep and goats. This soup was eaten by shepherds; the one who ate the human intestines was said to be transformed into a wolf and locked into that state until the next ceremony nine years later. At that point, he would turn back into a human if during the interim his wolf form had not eaten any human flesh.

In Scandinavia, wolf legends often related to the fierceness of warriors, with the most savage fighters having the appearance of wolves. In ancient illustrations, human figures might be depicted with the heads of bears or wolves. Wolfskin belts were thought to be required for a man or woman to turn into a wolf, and these articles were listed in the records of some witchcraft trials as evidence of evil. Stories of werewolves in Europe were first recorded during the Middle Ages. One of the most infamous of these was in France, where a man known as Gilles Garnier was said to have killed and eaten the bodies of many children. Witnesses reported him as assuming the form of either human or wolf at different times.

The phenomenon of humans changing into animals was not confined to wolves. People also reportedly changed into dogs and foxes. Usually linked to satanic or pagan rituals, accused practitioners were sometimes said to don a wolf skin (referred to as a wolf girdle in the fashion terminology of the period) and drink potent liquids that had magical powers. Incantations might also be invoked, including this spell:

"Make me a werewolf! Make me a man-eater!
Make me a werewolf! Make me a woman-eater!
Make me a werewolf! Make me a child-eater!
I pine for blood! Human blood!
Great Wolf spirit! Give it me and
Heart, body and soul, I am yours!"

The first record of the word werewolf was in religious writings of King Cnut, who lived from 1017 to 1035 A.D. By at least 1584, the word lycanthropia had been coined to "officially" cover the phenomenon, but at this point there was already some doubt as to whether it was a reality or merely a delusion. Reginald Scot, in his *The Discoverie of Witchcraft*, first suggested that it might be a malady of the mind rather than the body, a disease he called Lupina melancholia.

England's King James I wrote in 1597 "men have thought themselves verrie woolfes." He was not altogether convinced of a supernatural force behind this concept, for he also wrote "But to tell you simplie my opinion in this, if anie such thing hath bene, I take it to have proceeded but of a naturall super-abundance of Melancholie, which as wee reade, that it hath made some thinke themselves Pitchers, and some horses, and some one kinde of beast or other."

Widespread belief in werewolves manifested itself in physical signs that supposedly gave away the secret to those who knew what to look for. A superstition in Sicily, Denmark, France, Germany, and Scotland, for instance, was that the sign of a werewolf was heavy eyebrows that met across the brow. In some traditional Christian cultures, children born on Christmas day were said to be doomed to be werewolves because they had caused an affront to God by being born on the birthday of the Christchild. Babies born with teeth might also become werewolves, as were infants born feet first. People with hairy palms were suspect, as well as those with pointed ears or a loping walk.

As Christianity spread and became the dominant religion in Europe, so too did the concept of the werewolf as being evil, the antithesis of God. But even in the Middle Ages, the heyday of wolf-changing, rumor and suspicion were much more widespread than actual accusations. Court records from the 1500s and 1600s, when witchcraft was most actively pursued as a crime, show few cases of

"The traces left are indeed numerous enough, and though perhaps like the dodo or the dinormis, [sic. dinornis, or moa, an extinct bird] the werewolf may have become extinct in our age, yet he has left his stamp on classic antiquity, he has trodden deep in Northern snows, has ridden rough-shod over the mediaevals, and has howled amongst Oriental sepulchres. He belonged to a bad breed, and we are quite content to be freed from his and his kindred, the vampire and the ghoul. Yet who knows! We may be a little too hasty in concluding that he is extinct. He may still prowl in Abyssinian forests, range still over Asiatic steppes, and be found howling dismally in some padded room of a Hanwell or a Bedlam."
— Sabine Baring-Gould
The Book of Werewolves, 1865

werewolves being tried. In most regions of France, a single case at most was typical; in the German territories and the Holy Roman Empire, only a few cases were recorded.

The remnants of this mania, however, still exist in modern society, but are usually not connected to Christian beliefs. Medical records report several cases in recent years of individuals who exhibited episodes during which they believed they were wolves, including behavior typical of wolves such as howling and eating raw meat. Medical science, while it has no definitive answer to the forces which cause such abnormal behavior, suggests that this mental state may be related to schizophrenia. Looking back at the history of the werewolf phenomena in light of modern understandings of mental illness, children and adults who were accused of possession by animal spirits could have suffered from schizophrenia, the effects of hallucinogenic compounds, epilepsy, or autism.

WOLF MEDICINE

"The presence of hunters and Indian camps draws packs of wolves. These animals find excellent protection in the tall prairie grass and in the dense forests and are hunted but little or none at all. And since they rarely attack horses or people, nothing is done to hinder their increase, which is greatly favored by nature." — Duke of Württemberg
Travels in North America 1822–24

One early translation of an Aztec inscription described a medicine made from wolves' livers as a cure for melancholia. A sharpened wolf bone was also described as a therapeutic instrument if used to prick the breast. Pliny the Elder, a Greek who lived from 23 A.D. to 79 A.D., recommended the use of a wolf's tooth to relieve the pain of teething in infants, the tooth rubbed over the gums. As a cure for arthritis, another early Greek physician suggested soaking in a solution prepared by boiling whole wolves in oil. In medieval France, it was suggested one wear a wolf's tooth around the neck on a string to prevent nightmares.

Wolves were exploited by some tribes as a source of meat and hides. The Jicarilla Apaches made sleeping robes from wolf skins, sewing together four skins to produce a robe the same size as one made from a buffalo. Such a robe was thought to impart to the sleeper the strength and stamina of the animal it came from. Pawnees were said to use wolfskin blankets on their mules as a protection against predation. White or black skins might have particular power, and could also be used as an emblem or rank for a chief. One ancient cure for people infected with rabies from an animal bite was to don the hide of a wolf.

In order to keep the wolves away from a field, an ancient Roman prescription was to capture a wolf, break its legs, stab it deeply with a knife, and bury its body where it was killed after sprinkling the blood around the perimeter of the field.

The head of a wolf could be worn by a person in order to increase their courage, according to an ancient Sicilian belief. Sicilians also believed that shoes made of wolf skins were ideal for children in order to make them strong and brave when they grew up. In other parts of Europe, also, wolf-skin shoes were desirable to promote bravery.

Among the ancient Anglo-Saxons, wolves could also provide cosmetic usefulness. Their medicinal formulas included the following directive. "To remove ugly marks from the face, smear with wolf's blood, for it taketh away all marks."

A cow that suddenly startles and runs may be said to have a "wolf under the skin" or "wolf in the tail." The cure: make a cut in the cow's skin or tail and pour in some salt and pepper.

TAXONOMY

"The wolves of North America are much less than those which are met with in other parts of the world. They have, however, in common with the rest of their species, a wildness in their looks and a fierceness in their eyes; notwithstanding which they are far from being so ravenous as the European wolves, nor will they ever attack a man, except they have accidentally fed on the flesh of those slain in battle. When they herd together, as they often do in winter, they make a hideous and terrible noise. In these parts there are two kinds; one of which is of a fallow colour, the other of a dun, inclining to black."

— Jonathan Carver, 1766–1768

The first canids are thought to have developed from other carnivores between three and five million years ago. At least a few distinctive periods in this development have been noted, ancestral stages that included dog-like carnivores with many of the physical traits of modern canines. About one million years ago, the canids split into distinctive groups, including the separate species of coyotes and wolves, and for the first time creating animals similar in appearance to modern wolves.

At least according to the latest theories, both coyotes and wolves were originally native to this hemisphere, the New World. Migration throughout various periods of severe climate change brought wolves to Europe and Asia, but also allowed later generations to migrate back. One branch of the wolf evolutionary tree that came from South America was the dire wolf, a now extinct species of wolf that ranged in size from about the same size as the modern gray wolf to a much larger beast, the largest member of the dog family known to have existed. Dire wolves migrated throughout North America and existed at the same time and range as the earliest forms of gray wolves.

The dire wolf, now extinct, existed at the same time as the gray wolf, but was often larger in size.

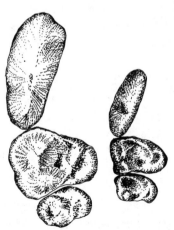

The teeth on the far left are from the fossilized remains of a dire wolf. On the right are the same teeth from a modern gray wolf.

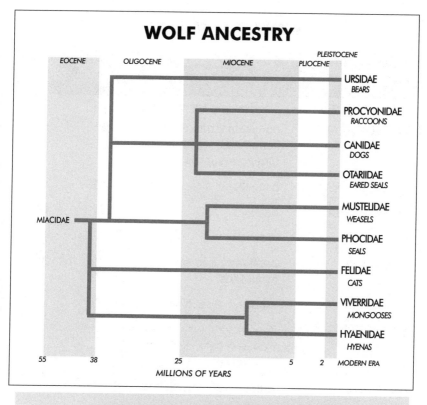

WOLF ANCESTRY

| EOCENE | OLIGOCENE | MIOCENE | PLIOCENE | PLEISTOCENE |

URSIDAE
BEARS

PROCYONIDAE
RACCOONS

CANIDAE
DOGS

OTARIIDAE
EARED SEALS

MUSTELIDAE
WEASELS

PHOCIDAE
SEALS

FELIDAE
CATS

VIVERRIDAE
MONGOOSES

HYAENIDAE
HYENAS

MIACIDAE

55   38   25   5   2   MODERN ERA

MILLIONS OF YEARS

SCIENTIFIC CLASSIFICATION

KINGDOM • Animals

PHYLUM • Chordata

CLASS • Mammals

ORDER • Carnivores

FAMILY • Canines (*Canidae*)

GENUS • Dogs (*Canis*)

SPECIES • Gray and Red wolves

WORLD MAMMALS

ORDER	DESCRIPTION	No. of SPECIES	No. of FAMILIES
MONOTREMES	platypus and spiny anteater	3	2
MARSUPIALIA	opossums, bandicoots, kangaroos, wombats, and other marsupials	265	15
INSECTIVORA	hedgehogs, moles, shrews	406	9
CHIROPTERA	bats	879	18
RODENTIA	rodents	1625	31
EDENTATA	anteaters, tree sloths, armadillos	28	3
LAGOMORPHA	rabbits, hares, pikas	60	2
CARNIVORA	dogs, foxes, wolves, seals, weasels, cats, and other carnivores	266	9
CETACEA	whales, dolphins, porpoises	76	10
PROBOSCIDEA	elephants	2	1
SIRENIA	dugongs, manatees	4	2
PERISSODACTYLA	horses, zebras, tapirs, rhinoceroses	16	3
ARTOPDACTYLA	antelope, deer, gazelles, giraffe, pigs, hippos, and other ruminants	185	9
PRIMATES	lemurs, monkeys, apes, and humans	199	15

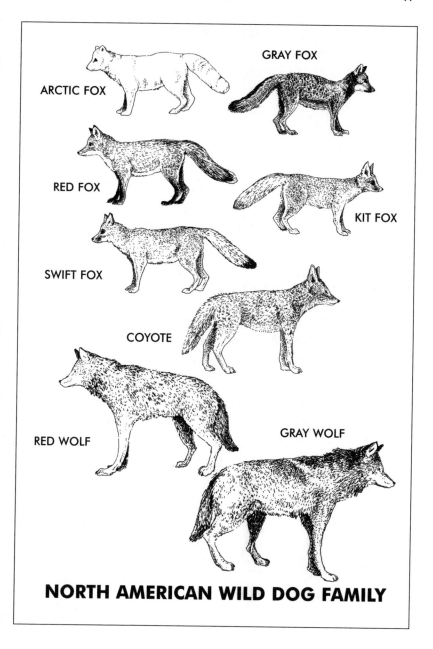

ARCTIC FOX

GRAY FOX

RED FOX

KIT FOX

SWIFT FOX

COYOTE

RED WOLF

GRAY WOLF

NORTH AMERICAN WILD DOG FAMILY

THE FAMILY

Wolves are one of thirty-five species of the world Canid family. The wild dogs vary greatly in appearance, with the fennec — an African fox — at the smallest extreme in size and the gray wolf at the other. Attributes that are shared by wild dogs include:

- erect ears
- long, narrow muzzles
- bushy tails
- forefeet with five toes each (fifth toe is a dewclaw)
- hindfeet with four toes
- all toes are nonretractable
- long legs in proportion to body size
- forty-two teeth, twenty over twenty-two
- large, distinctive canine teeth
- specialized sets of carnassial teeth
  (upper premolars and lower molar used for severing food)
- acute senses of sight, hearing, smell
- regulate body temperature by panting
- omnivorous diet

In North America, members of the wild dog family include: coyotes, red foxes, gray foxes, kit foxes, swift foxes, arctic foxes, gray wolves and red wolves.

THE GENUS OF CANIS

GOLDEN JACKAL

SIMIEN JACKAL

BLACK-BACKED JACKAL

SIDE-STRIPED JACKAL

RED WOLF

COYOTE

GRAY WOLF

DOMESTIC DOG

WORLD WOLVES

Wolves are widely dispersed throughout the world but are all closely related members of the gray wolf species. The red wolves are found only in the southern part of North America. World wolf sub-species are:

- European wolf (*Canis lupus lupus*), Europe and Eurasia in forest habitat
- Caucasian wolf or steppe wolf (*Canis lupus cubanensis* or *Canis lupus campestris*), Central Asia in desert and steppe habitats
- Arabian wolf (*Canis lupus arabs*), Southern Arabia
- Tundra wolf or Turukhan wolf (*Canis lupus albus*), throughout Eurasia in tundra habitat
- Japanese wolf (*Canis lupus hattai*), northern islands of Japan; may be extinct
- Tibetan wolf (*Canis lupus laniger*), Central Asia
- Indian wolf (*Canis lupus pallipes*), Southwestern Asia

Scientists have not yet made conclusive classifications of the number of subspecies of wolves but it is likely to be about 40, including as many as 24 in North America. The only areas of the globe where wolves have not been present are the continent of Africa and regions of extreme dryness and wetness, deserts and rain forests. Because of an almost universal reputation as a nasty beast, wolves have been eliminated or severely reduced in numbers over much of this range.

NORTH AMERICAN WOLVES

Wolves in North America exist as several distinct subspecies, although there is no general agreement about how these subspecies may be classified. In past years, taxonomists divided North American wolves into as many as 24 distinct subspecies, including several that have become extinct only in this century. While wolves of one or more groups may interbreed with those of another group, it is currently believed that little such interbreeding is common.

The separation of groups is a natural outcome of how wolves live as well as their preferred habitats. A strong and continuing link exists between each group of wolves and their major prey. Because the prey animals of wolves are mostly ungulates — deer, moose, elk, caribou — and these herd animals live within distinct environments, the wolves also tend to stick to these environmental ranges. Subtle differences in communication and behavior are inherited and learned within each wolf group, adding an additional barrier that may keep subspecies from mingling, but these factors may be overridden by the pressures created from expanding human cultures. But mingling has occurred throughout history between wolves and other members of the dog family. Interbreeding with domestic dogs and coyotes was common, if irregular.

During prolonged periods of stress, starvation, or environmental change, wolves may be forced to alter their territory or hunting behavior, pushing them into closer contact with other wolf groups. Wolves, like the coyote, are intelligent and opportunistic and are more likely to take advantage of change than other animals. Especially in recent centuries, changes related to human populations have had a tremendous impact on the natural ranges of wolves in North America. Most recently, the widespread hunting of buffalo on the western plains and the large-scale introduction of cattle ranching has had much impact.

For practical purposes, there may only be three truly different types of wolves on the continent: the red wolf and two varieties of gray wolves, timber wolves and tundra wolves. Of these, only the red wolf is visibly and noticeably different, being much smaller and confined to a range sharply removed from the others. But even the red wolf classification is open to debate, with some biologists supporting the theory that this wolf is merely a natural hybrid of gray wolves and coyotes.

SCIENTIFIC HERITAGE

The North American gray wolf was once considered a group consisting of more than 40 different subspecies. According to the formerly accepted scientific descriptions, some of these subspecies included:

- *Canis lupus hudsonicus.* Range: Canada, coastal areas of Hudson Bay and James Bay
- *Canis lupus lycaon.* Boreal type — Range: Canada, boreal forests in northern and central areas. Algonquin type — Range: Canada, deciduous-coniferous forests. Tweed type — Range: Canada, southern fringes of Algonquin type
- *Canis lupus crassodo.* Also known as the Vancouver Island wolf. Range: Vancouver Island, B.C.
- *Canis lupus ligoni.* Range: Alaska
- *Canis lupus tundrarum.* Range: Alaska
- *Canis lupus alces.* Range: Alaska
- *Canis lupus crassodon.* Range: British Columbia
- *Canis lupus columbianus.* Range: British Columbia and the Yukon
- *Canis lupus pambasileus.* Range: British Columbia and the Yukon
- *Canis lupus irremotus.* Range: British Columbia, Yukon, Alberta
- *Canis lupus nubilus.* Range: Canada: Alberta, Saskatchewan, Manitoba. USA: Minnesota
- *Canis lupus orion.* Range: Canada: Newfoundland, Northwest Territories
- *Canis lupus irremotus.* Range: USA: northwestern states, northern Rocky Mountains

RANGE

"As one views and considers the vast continental range of the gray wolf, one realizes that it is equally at home in the semitropics of lowland Texas and on the rugged islands of the Polar Sea. It is found everywhere within the territory marked — open plains, dense forests, rolling uplands, or matted canebrakes — competent and triumphant, except in the water, on thirsty, burning desert of the Southwest, and among the wind-swept peaks of Goatland..."
— Ernest Thompson Seton, 1925

Wolves once roamed over most of the North American continent. With the exception of extremely arid and extremely wet regions — deserts and rain forests — wolves were at home from the arctic to central Mexico, from the Pacific coast to the Atlantic coast.

Even under the most favorable conditions in North America, wolf populations in a given area are usually not very large. A typical density might be one wolf per 10 square miles. In one unique island habitat — Coronation Island, Alaska — wolves have been reported at a density of one wolf per three square miles. At the other extreme — Ontario, Canada — there are between one and two hundred square miles per wolf. The average wolf density is about one per 10 square miles (26 square kilometers).

In North America, there are few areas left where wolves are completely free from interference from human populations. In the past, their populations were able to increase rapidly if there was little interference such as hunting or trapping, and there was an abundance of prey. One study of a protected area in Alaska indicated that a wolf population can increase by at least 20 percent per year, but only if it has not already established a maximum concentration. Natural controls on wolf populations other than hunting and trap-

ORIGINAL RANGE OF THE GRAY WOLF

ping can include extreme weather conditions, the abundance of prey, and the presence of disease. Under natural conditions, wolf populations may fluctuate in size from year to year — often linked to the availability of food — but over time an average population size is maintained.

A long-running study of wolves on an isolated island in Lake Superior (Isle Royale National Park) has shown the relationship between predator and prey over time, with one population increasing or decreasing in response to the other. But if a wolf population is not confined to a limited geographic region such as an island, the influences are more complex. With room to roam, individual or groups of wolves may leave an established hunting territory in search of mates or new sources of food.

ORIGINAL RANGE OF THE RED WOLF

Unlike the gray wolf, the traditional range of the red wolf extended only from central Texas on the west, through Georgia and Florida to the Atlantic coast. On the north, it extended up through the Mississippi River valley to central Illinois and central Indiana. The present range is six counties in southeastern Texas and one parish in southwestern Louisiana, with experimental reintroduction programs underway in several other states. As of mid-1995, the total population of red wolves — including those in captivity in zoos — was 289.

WOLF SPECIES

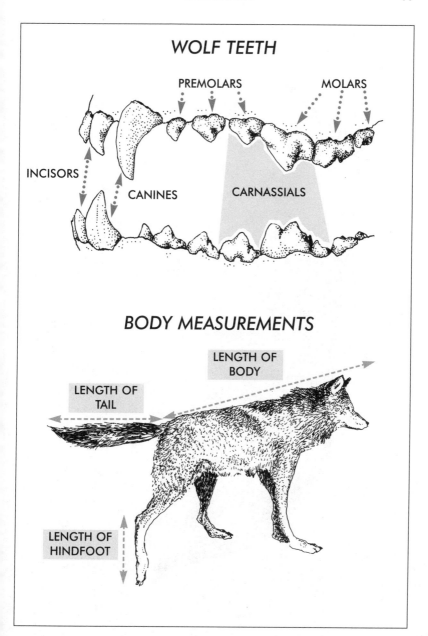

WOLF TEETH

PREMOLARS

MOLARS

INCISORS

CANINES

CARNASSIALS

BODY MEASUREMENTS

LENGTH OF BODY

LENGTH OF TAIL

LENGTH OF HINDFOOT

GRAY WOLF
Canis lupus

VITAL STATISTICS

OFFICIAL NAME	Gray wolf *Canis lupus*
COMMON NAMES	Gray wolf, timber wolf, arctic wolf, lobo
SUBSPECIES	*Canis lupus arctos, Canis lupus baileyi, Canis lupus lycaon, Canis lupus nubilus, Canis lupus occidentalis* (proposed) 24 subspecies traditionally recognized
COMPARISON	Larger than coyotes or domestic dogs. Compared to coyote: ears shorter and rounder, muzzle broader, head larger and wider, longer legs, larger paws. Compared to red wolf: larger in size, natural range is farther north.
DESCRIPTION	Largest North American wolf. Color can be white or black but is most often mixture of shades of brown, tans, and gray; muzzle usually lighter in color; longer, shaggy hair around neck and shoulders forming mane; large, rounded ears, usually held erect; males larger than females.

HEAD+BODY LENGTH	39–80 " 99–203 cm	**TAIL LENGTH**	14.5–18 " 37–46 cm
WEIGHT	50–130 lbs 23–59 kg	**HEIGHT AT SHOULDER**	26–36 " 66–91 cm
		HINDFOOT LENGTH	9.5–11.6 " 24–29 cm
TEETH	42 teeth I 3/3, C 1/1, PM 4/5, M 2/3		

HOME RANGE	Original range included most of North America. Current range is most of Canada, Alaska, parts of Minnesota, Idaho, Montana, and Washington; reintroduced in Yellowstone Park (Montana).
HABITAT	Plains, forests, tundra.
FOOD	Caribou, white-tailed deer, mule deer, Dall's sheep, bighorn sheep, mountain goat, muskox, elk, bison, moose, small mammals, birds, fish, carrion.
BREEDING	Mating: January-March. Alpha males usually mate with alpha females. One litter per year; one litter per pack is typical, reproduction is generally by alpha pair. Gestation period: 63 days. Litter size 3–12, average size 6. Birthing: April-June. Birth weight: 12–16 ounces (350-450 gms). Weaning: 5 weeks. Sexual maturity: 2 years.
VOCAL CALL	Distinctive howling, alone or in unison with other wolves; barking; growling.
HABITS	Usually lives and travels in packs; dens used for raising young; distinctive hierarchy among pack members with an "alpha" wolf or wolf pair. Complex communications among wolves includes facial, tail, and body signals as well as scent marking. Primary complaints: destruction of domestic animals, especially cattle and sheep.

RANGE FOR GRAY WOLF
Approximate current range. For natural range of gray
wolf, see page 49.

RED WOLF
Canis rufus

VITAL STATISTICS

OFFICIAL NAME	Red wolf *Canis rufus*
COMMON NAMES	Red wolf
SUBSPECIES	*Canis rufus rufus, Canis rufus gregoryi*
COMPARISON	Generally larger than most coyotes or domestic dogs. Compared to coyote: ears shorter and rounder, muzzle broader, head larger and wider, longer legs, larger paws. Compared to gray wolf: smaller in size, natural range is farther south, ears usually held at an angle away from the head.
DESCRIPTION	Smallest North American wolf, about the size of a coyote; large ears; coloring is mixture of reds, grays, browns, and blacks; muzzle color usually predominately light or white; ears held at an angle away from the head.

HEAD+BODY LENGTH	55–65 " 140–165 cm	**TAIL LENGTH**	13–16 " 33–41 cm
WEIGHT	45–60 lbs 20–27 kg	**HEIGHT AT SHOULDER**	15–16 " 38–41 cm
		HINDFOOT LENGTH	8-10 " 20–25 cm
TEETH	42 teeth I 3/3, C 1/1, PM 4/5, M 2/3		

HOME RANGE	Originally found from central Texas on the west through Georgia and Florida to the Atlantic coast, north through the Mississippi River valley to central Illinois and central Indiana; present natural range is six counties in southeastern Texas and one parish in southwestern Louisiana. Reintroduced in North Carolina, South Carolina, Mississippi, and Florida.
HABITAT	Prairies, forests, swamps.
FOOD	White-tailed deer, swamp rabbit, cottontail rabbit, nutria, rice rat, cotton rat, muskrat, raccoon, insects, crustaceans, mollusks, fruit.
BREEDING	Breeding: Mating: January-February. One litter per year. Gestation period 63 days. Litter size: 3-4. Birthing March-April. Birth weight: unknown. Weaning: 5 weeks. Sexual maturity: 2 years.
VOCAL CALL	Howling more like coyote than gray wolf; barking; growling.
HABITS	Usually lives and travels in pairs; dens used for raising young.

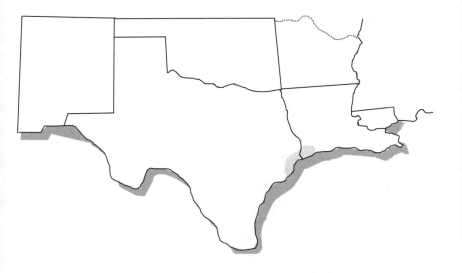

RANGE FOR RED WOLF

For natural range of red wolf, see page 50.

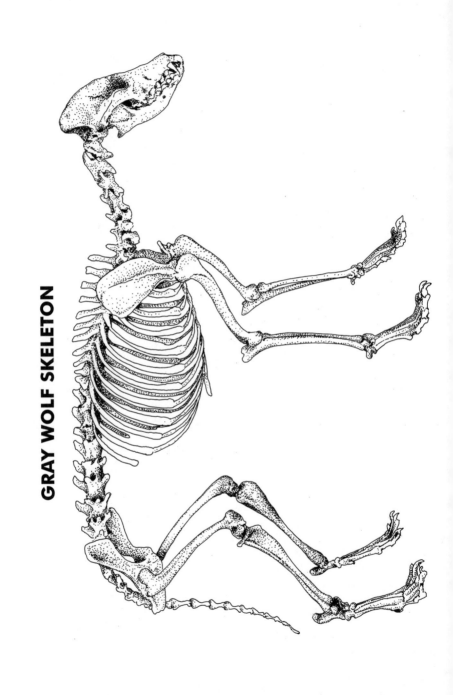

GRAY WOLF SKELETON

GRAY WOLF SKULL
(*Canis lupus*)

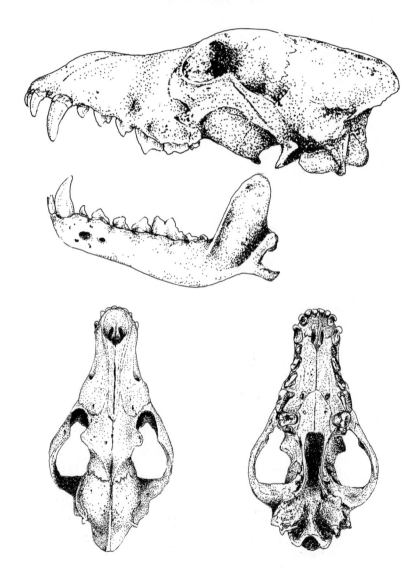

ANATOMY

"The Wolf ... has his senses in great perfection. He smells a carcass at the distance of more than a league; he also perceives living animals a great way off, and follows them a long time upon the scent. Whenever he leaves the wood, he always takes care to go out against the wind. When just come to its extremity, he stops to examine, by its smell, on all sides, the emanations that may come either from his enemy or his prey, which he very nicely distinguishes."
— Georges Louis Leclerc Buffon, 1879

SIZE

The wolf is the largest member of the dog family. Individuals may range from 63 to 77 inches in length and weigh from 40 to 170 pounds. Most adult wolves weigh between 60 and 100 pounds, with the average weight close to 100 pounds. In general, larger size is more common in the northern parts of the North American range. The red wolf is an exception, with an average weight of only 40 pounds. Adult males are generally 15–20 percent larger than adult females. The largest wolf on record weighed 175 pounds (killed by a hunter in 1939 in eastern Alaska).

WOLF SIZES

North American adult gray wolves vary in
size from more than 150 pounds
to less than 100 pounds.

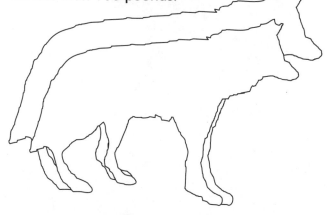

Gray wolves (in rear) are typically
larger than red wolves.

COLOR VARIATIONS

COLOR

Wolves exhibit a variety of colors in their fur, rarely showing conformity, even in the same family pack. Colors vary from all white to all black, the extreme phases of coloration in this animal. Although like all mammals a wolf may be an albino — physically lacking any pigment in its fur — light-colored wolves are almost always that color because of a specific pigment rather than from albinism. Animals that are albino may vary from partial to complete, with patches of white fur at the one extreme to a complete lack of color in the fur at the other. Completely albino mammals also usually have pink eyes and pink tissue in all unfurred areas, including the paws and nose.

The most common colors found in wolves are grays and browns. A single wolf typically has more than one color in its coat. A grizzled pattern is common with bands of lighter and darker color on the hair creating a "salt and pepper" effect. Most wolves also have lighter coloring on the belly, the lower jaw, the underside of the tail, and the inner surface of the legs. Guard hairs may have more than one color, with the tips being lighter or darker than the shaft. As wolves age, some hairs — particularly on the tail and snout — may develop white tips.

Red wolves have color variation similar to gray wolves, but are more likely to have reddish tones in their fur. Red wolves, despite their name, may be extremely pale in color or almost black, and are often confused with coyotes because of their similar coloration and size.

Coloring on the head is a distinctive feature for most wolves. Even with animals exhibiting a uniform light or dark color, these distinctive markings can usually be seen. Dark lines surround the eyes and darker markings outline the ears. The longer hairs around the sides of the head — almost forming a mane — are often a lighter color. These color variations can help emphasize expressions that are used to communicate.

Black wolves were originally thought to be part of a distinctive subspecies of the North American wolf. In reality, a black color phase may occur in all types of North American wolves, but is most common in the gray wolf. Larger numbers of black wolves have been reported in some geographic regions.

EYES

The eyes of all members of the dog family — including wolves — are primarily adapted for spotting prey. Eyes in most predators, including the dog family, are set forward to the front of the head, concentrating vision ahead of the animal. An added advantage to this type of eye placement is more room in the skull for the brain, an advantage that could have been instrumental in the development of the wolf's superior intelligence. The brain, in general, tends to be larger in animals that have greater reliance on eyesight because these types of brains require a larger visual-processing capacity, a physically larger brain. Or it may be that an increase in intelligence predisposed animals to hunt prey. In any case, prey animals such as rabbits and deer have eyes set more to the sides of the head, the better to provide a wider range of visual warning against predators, and compared to predators, have a smaller brain size in comparison to their body.

Forward-set eyes also create the best possible circumstances for binocular vision. This visual facility allows an animal to accurately determine the distance between itself and an object. Binocular vision also concentrates a field of attention in a smaller area, giving an animal better coordination of movement and accuracy when striking at prey. For a predator, this can make the difference between survival and death by starvation. One drawback to binocular vision, however, is that in most predator species, hunting activities are most productive when there is the most light, making most predators more efficient in daylight — or diurnal — conditions. A few predator species are exceptions to this rule and are completely nocturnal, and some, including the wolf, are considered arrhythmic, active during both daylight and nighttime phases.

No animal can see in complete darkness. But in the natural world there is almost always at least a low level of light, illumination coming from the moon or stars even on the darkest nights. Canine eyes are adapted to work well in conditions of low light, giving wolves the ability to be efficient hunters even after the sun sets. Because they traditionally hunt at night, wolves and other dogs have eyes containing mostly rods, the sensitive visual cells in the retina.

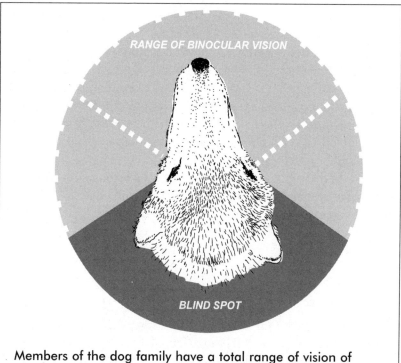

Members of the dog family have a total range of vision of about 270 degrees, with binocular vision of about 100 degrees.

About 95 percent of a wolf's eye is rods. The wolf eye lacks a fovea, the central part of an eye that is adapted to pick up the smallest detail. The fovea is an area of the retina that has a larger concentration of cells to receive light signals. The result for the wolf and other dogs is vision that may miss extremely fine details. Human eyes, on the other hand, include foveas, giving them at least one visual advantage over dogs.

Wolf eyes have a yellow pigment and the pupils are black. An animal's mood may be reflected in the size of the pupil, with the pupil expanding or contracting in response to fear, nervousness, curiosity, or aggressiveness. The larger the pupil, the more intense the mood. Wolves do not have a full range of color vision, but most colors are distinctive to them, including red, yellow, green, and blue.

Like many other predators, the wolf relies on its vision to detect, chase, and capture prey. Wolf eyes are capable of detecting movement and identifying prey at distances of more than one hundred feet, with the extreme limit probably less than one hundred yards.

Wolf puppies are born sightless, with their eyes closed. When they are 11–15 days old, they begin opening their eyes but have limited vision for several weeks.

Wolves use eye contact as a means of establishing authority and dominance among other wolves. Dominant wolves seek direct eye contact and expect submissive behavior in response. To a wolf, staring is more than impolite, it may be considered a threat.

EARS

The ears of a wolf are one of its most distinctive features, erect and prominent near the top of its head. Wolf ears are rounded and smaller in proportion to the size of the head than those of the coyote, with which it is often confused. The position of the ears places

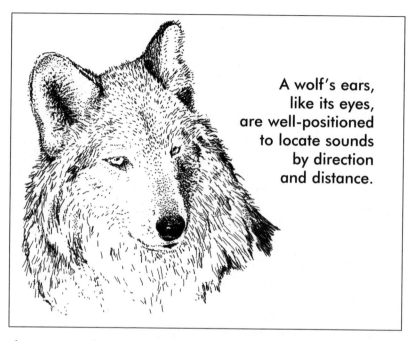

A wolf's ears, like its eyes, are well-positioned to locate sounds by direction and distance.

them in an ideal position for capturing sound. Extending up to three inches above the head, the ears are not blocked by any part of the head. Muscles and connective tissue allow the wolf a wide degree of movement for each ear, and each ear can be moved independently of the other. Like miniature radio receivers, the ears can be shifted to the best position to identify the location of a sound. With both ears pointed toward a sound source, the wolf has an additional tracking capability, the ability to gauge distances from its head to the sound source, similar to the binocular effect of its vision.

Wolves, like all dogs, can hear sounds in a greater range of frequencies than humans. The high part of this range is about 26,000 cycles per second (26 kHz). Their hearing is also more acute—able to detect the faintest of noises and sounds at a distance of up to ten miles in open terrain. This acute hearing may also be put to work at much shorter distances, pinpointing the scurrying of rodents under a blanket of snow.

Wolf puppies are born deaf, their ears closed to sounds from the outside world. They begin hearing within a few weeks of birth.

PAWS

For an animal which is almost constantly on the move, paws are a critical feature of the body. Wolf paws are large and strong, able to carry the animal long distances, grip the terrain in a wide variety of weather and ground conditions, and perform actions such as holding prey, burying food caches, and digging burrows.

The front paw has five toes with claws, with one a short claw on the inside of the foot, referred to as the dewclaw. The back paw has only four toes and claws. These claws are fixed and cannot be retracted like those of the cat family. The front paws are larger than the rear paws. A large adult wolf paw can be 5 inches in length and almost 5 inches in width. Rear paws may measure only about 3 inches in either dimension. Toe pads are oval to round in shape. The red wolf has paws that are relatively hairless but the gray wolf's coat extends over the entire paw, including hairs between the toes. This hair helps protect the skin against freezing temperatures and surfaces.

In North America, wolf traps have frequently been responsible for complete or partial dismemberment of toes, toe pads, and paws. Wolves with missing foot parts may suffer disease or attack from other wolves who sense weakness, and they suffer from a diminished ability to pursue prey. Anecdotal evidence from decades of trapping and wolf hunting indicates that wolves with missing foot parts are also likely to be involved in attacks on domesticated animals. These prey — primarily cattle and sheep — are easier to capture and kill than the wolves' traditional wild food sources and may

LIFE-SIZED FRONT PAWPRINT

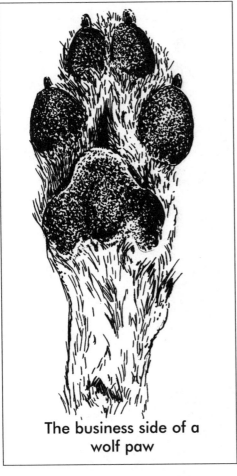

The business side of a
wolf paw

be preyed upon because of a diminished capacity to hunt.

The wide footprint of the wolf paw gives it stability and support on most surfaces. In the snow and ice, this may be a significant advantage for capturing prey, but in extreme snow conditions, this paw design is not enough to prevent a serious loss of mobility. Soft, loose snow that hinders the wolf's movement often influences its choice of travel route; in many snowy habitats, wolves frequently opt for frozen lake surfaces, man-made trails, or routes cleared by the passage of other animals. Historical reports indicate that many wolves die during winters with large amounts of snowfall, a loss not because of cold but from lack of mobility.

Wolf paws are also thought to have evolved a unique method of blood circulation that keeps their feet from freezing in cold weather. Before the blood reaches the outer layers of tissue, it is precooled, lessening the difference in temperature inside and outside the body. No other member of the dog family has this feature.

TEETH

Teeth make up the business end of the wolf, its necessary tools for survival as a predator. The wolf species has 42 teeth of four types, each type designed to perform a specific task. The largest teeth are appropriately called canines, long and fang-like and used to grab and puncture prey. Incisors are sharp and used like chisels, cutting away pieces of food. Premolars also strip away food with a cutting action. Molars are designed to crush and can pulverize bones to expose marrow. Unlike most other mammals, none of the wolf's teeth are designed well for chewing, and eating is mostly comprised of swallowing whole chunks of meat.

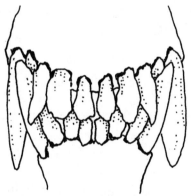

FRONT VIEW OF WOLF JAW

Large canine teeth in both the upper and lower jaws arm a wolf with efficient natural tools for grabbing prey and defending itself.

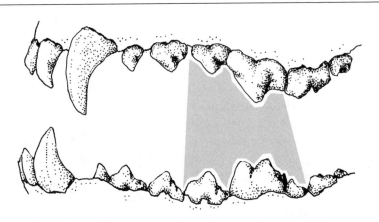

The carnassial teeth are specially adapted for efficient use by predators. The combination of the upper and lower teeth in this unit function like a pair of scissors, allowing a wolf to slice off chunks of tissue from its prey.

The combination of the last premolar and the first molar work in tandem to create a shearing effect on tissue, the upper and lower teeth working together like scissors. These teeth are sometimes referred to as carnassial teeth — or flesh teeth — a term referring to shearing rather than chewing. The carnassial teeth allow wolves to cut off chunks of tissue for swallowing.

But most of the initial biting power comes from the canine teeth, with about two-thirds of their length supported by jaw and gums. A typical adult canine tooth can be almost 2.5 inches in length. These canines are used as attack weapons, puncturing hide, tissue, and bone during the initial assault. Wolves have been observed hanging onto large game such as elk and moose with their canines while the animals violently attempt to shake them off.

Wolf teeth are powered by jaws and muscles that have tremendous power. Although no scientific measurements have ever been made of this power, it is estimated that the jaws of a wolf can exert a force up to 1,500 pounds per square inch, greater than the power of the largest domesticated dog. This bite power is an effective method of disabling and killing prey animals. In some cases, a single bite can sever the spine of the prey. Many eye-witnesses to wolf attacks on animals have reported this biting power in action, with numerous descriptions of the unique sound of these powerful teeth snapping sharply together. In the wild and among livestock, unsuccessful wolf attacks often leave a visual reminder, the neatly severed tails of the intended victims.

Wolf teeth, being much in use, can suffer from wear and abuse over time. The older the wolf, the greater the wear. Incisors are the most likely teeth to suffer from breakage. Once a wolf's teeth have deteriorated, it may alter its feeding habits, switching from primarily hunting and killing live prey to the scavenging of already dead animals. In earlier eras when wolves still populated most of the western states, trappers sometimes called animals with broken or worn teeth "gummer wolves," or "smooth-mouthed wolves." And like wolves with paws missing or damaged from traps, the crippling of the wolf's bite may influence it to select a more productive form of prey — livestock.

SENSE OF SMELL

The nose of the wolf may be its most acute sensory organ. Like all dogs, wolves are able to detect odors in extremely minute quantities, far exceeding the range of human beings. That the wolf nose can pick up the faintest scents is not just an advantage to its role as a predator; scent to wolves is like a second form of memory, enabling one wolf to identify another. Scent-marking — with urine and feces — is a standard form of communication between wolves,

Any source of strong odor, including carrion, may initiate scent-rolling behavior, one way wolves use to communicate with other wolves by sharing odors.

signaling territorial boundaries, aggression, pack identity, and sexual receptiveness.

When on the move, wolves punctuate their travel with scent marks every few minutes. Along regular routes and within specified territories, individual trees or rocks may be permanent scent posts, regularly marked during movement. When investigating odors, especially on other pack members, wolves exhibit a "snuffling" behavior, using their nose to thoroughly track over the surface of the face or through the fur.

When on the hunt, wolves can detect the scent of a prey animal from a distance of a few miles if the wind is in the right direction. According to some reports, wolves have been able to pick up the scent of a prey animal at even greater distances on occasion.

Wolves may use urine as a means of marking territory, to cover the scent of other wolves, and sometimes as a display of dominance.

FUR

Wolves, like many mammals, have three types of external hair: underhair, guard hair, and sensory hairs. The underhair is the hidden layer of insulating material that allows the animals to thrive even in the coldest climates. Underhair is thickly matted, much like the wool on a lamb, trapping air and forming an effective insulating barrier.

Guard hair is the longer visible hair that makes up the external coat of fur. Air pockets in the shaft of guard hairs add additional insulating capacity. The guard hairs around the neck and shoulders are longer than elsewhere on the body, up to 5 inches in length. When threatened, this hair can be erected almost like a mane, making the wolf appear larger.

Wolves shed their heavy fur in the spring, growing new hair for the warm season that is often lighter in color than their winter coat. The guard hairs of the summer coat are also shorter than the winter version. Shedding usually occurs in patches, with clumps of fur falling out in a ragged pattern. Erratic shedding may also affect the coat in times of stress or as a result of some diseases and parasites, most notably the mange mite. Adult female wolves will usually have darker hair around their nipples when pregnant or nursing. Some of this hair may also fall out during nursing.

Wolves in southern portions of their range may have thinner, shorter coats than wolves in more northern areas. The red wolf, with a home range geographically placed in a warmer climate in the southern part of the United States, has a coat with shorter, sparser hair than its northern cousins. Individual wolves in all parts of their

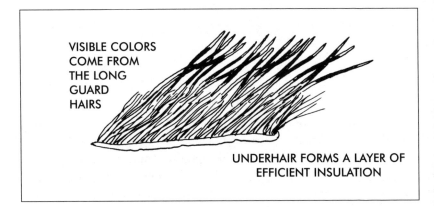

VISIBLE COLORS COME FROM THE LONG GUARD HAIRS

UNDERHAIR FORMS A LAYER OF EFFICIENT INSULATION

natural range may be affected with albinism, a hereditary condition that makes all or parts of their hair white. True albinos also have pink eyes. Most wolves that are light in color are not, however, true albinos, but simply have a naturally light-colored hair.

TAIL

The wolf's tail can be used as insulation against the cold, wrapped around the body while at rest to help conserve heat. Although the tail does not have much weight, it can also be used

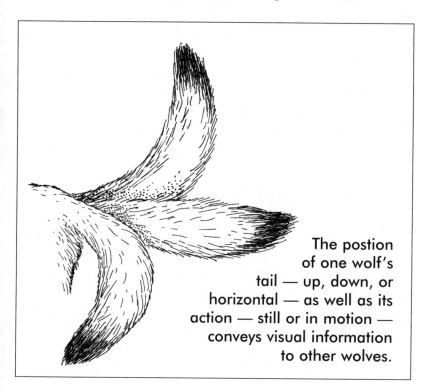

The postion of one wolf's tail — up, down, or horizontal — as well as its action — still or in motion — conveys visual information to other wolves.

as a counterbalance, helping to maintain balance during rapid changes in direction while running. Primarily, however, the tail serves as a means of communication. The position, attitude, and movement of the tail all signify specific moods to other wolves. Most of the time, wolves carry their tails low and to the rear. In contrast, domesticated dogs have a characteristic upward curl to their tails.

The tail is between 14.5 and 18 inches in length in adult wolves. As a general rule, the tail is less than half the length of the body and usually reaches no lower than the knee joint.

A wolf's tail is covered with long guard hairs, with colors repeating or similar to those found on the rest of its body. The tip of the tail in most wolves is darker than the rest of the tail and the underside is lighter. Older wolves often develop white-tipped hairs in their tails as they get older. Many wolf tails also feature a darker patch on the top near the base, a mark located at the site of the supracaudal gland. This gland has no proven function, but it is thought to secrete a distinctive scent used for communication with other wolves.

DIGESTIVE SYSTEM

Wolves have evolved to respond to changing food supplies, their digestive systems designed primarily for animal protein but capable of handling extremes in quantity and quality of food. From one year or one season to the next, the amount of food available can change dramatically. In order to survive, wolves have developed the instinct to eat as much food as possible when it is present, particularly if it follows a day or more of not eating. The result is gorging, the consumption of extremely large portions of prey. After gorging, however, wolves usually become sleepy and lethargic. Wolf hunters in a former era referred to wolves that gorged as "meat drunk" and wolves that had been gorging were often easy to approach and kill.

This distinctive eating habit has made "wolfish" a term suggesting greed, but in the case of wolves, it has less to do with avarice than survival. An experiment by Stanley Young, author of *Wolves of North America* (1944), indicated that wolves can eat about 20 percent of their body weight after a period of starvation. For a wolf that weighed 80 pounds, this would mean 16 pounds of meat.

The indiscriminate "wolfing" of food may include the entire body parts of some animals because of speed of consumption and the tendency for wolves to tear off and swallow whole pieces of their prey. Wolf stomachs examined in Alaska have been found to contain whole caribou tongues, kidneys, livers, ears, and chunks of hide that include the hair.

Wolves have molars, teeth which in other animals, primarily plant eaters, effectively grind food into smaller particles before swallowing. But wolf molars are not used in this fashion, food instead being gulped and swallowed in chunks and pieces. Their molars and tremendous jaw strength are instead used to crush bones to expose the nutritious marrow.

Rapid feeding is a survival mechanism for the wolf and its digestive system has adapted to process the ingested meat as quickly as possible. Almost as fast as the wolf can eat, its body can process the food into protein. In the wild, wolves may feed several times during a day when a carcass is available, with the food digested within a few hours each time.

Wolf feces can be produced as rapidly as their digestion system works, but it also changes in response to the content of what they are eating. From experiments with wolves in captivity, the result of such gorging behavior was, according to Stanley Young, "the passage of large quantities of exceedingly loose excreta of the consistency and color of melted licorice." The loose stools typically produced when they are gorging on fresh meat are the opposite of the feces produced when they ingest bone, skin, or connective tissue.

Scat — the term used by biologists to refer to animal feces — produced from this diet includes nondigestible material such as bone
fragments and hair. The intestines of the wolf are designed to
process this material without harming the intestines; the sharp and
potentially dangerous bits of bone are found in the center of wolf
scat, with hair and softer material on the outside. Wolf scat is cylin-
drical and from 1 to 1.5 inches in diameter.

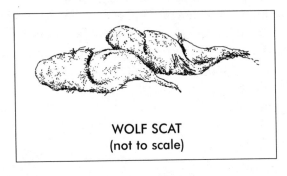

WOLF SCAT
(not to scale)

COMMUNICATION

"Speaking of the language of animals, the most thrilling as well as — to me — the most soul-stirring music I ever heard was the clear deep bass voice of a big gray wolf on a clear cold winter night rolling out over the ice-covered prairie."
— James R. Mead, 1859–1875

Wolves use their eyes, mouth, ears, tails, fur, body posture, urine, feces, and voices to communicate with other wolves. To humans, the most distinctive of these forms is their voice, a howl that throughout history has symbolized the mystery of the animal presence in nature.

Howling can occur at all times of the year, day or night, in groups or alone, and before or after a hunt. Wolves in captivity also howl. The most likely time for wolves to howl is during the evening or early morning hours. Alone or in groups, their howls can carry for up to ten miles and thus form an effective means of sending messages to other wolves. One wolf or pack might use the howl to reinforce territorial boundaries or link separated members of the same pack. But even where there are no neighboring wolves or scattered pack members, howling is a common behavior, representing unknown motivations. Because of their interest in playful behavior, some biologists believe this howling could sometimes be an expression with no practical consequence, serving just for pleasure. Because packs almost always join together in a howling chorus when one wolf begins to howl, it is also possible that it is an additional bonding behavior that strengthens the community of the pack.

In any case, the keen senses of the wolf allow it to identify other wolves by their voices. Young wolves first begin to display this behavior at about four weeks, howling along with their parents and other pack members. Measurements of single wolf howls indicate

"But after all, its an awfull thing to be living in the woods. Oh! them terrible wolves, if you were to hear them. I never got a wink of sleep the first fortennight. I'd be shockingly in dread, they'd spoil our tea party. Such yowling, and growling, and yelling, and pellmelling, as no Christian ever heard. They say it's hunting the deer they are. Set `em up with venzon the bastes!"

— Bridget Lacy, 1832

they may last from 1 second to more than 10 seconds and contain up to 12 harmonic overtones. A howling session averages about half a minute but may last for several minutes when a single wolf is involved; a howling session with more than one wolf lasts about a minute and a half on average. When separate wolves or wolf packs are engaged in howling sessions, they howl in a cycle that repeats about every forty minutes. Such choruses can continue throughout an entire night.

Howling is not uniform, with each wolf having its own distinctive howl and often a variation each time it howls. Howls usually start with lower tones and build up to higher pitches. Wolves in concert howl with complimentary pitches, forming unique chords that harmonize.

Although gray wolves do not bark as often as domesticated dogs, they do use barks as another form of communication. Barks may be used to signal an alarm or to challenge another wolf. Growls are another form of challenge as well as threat, usually part of an aggressive display. Whimpering, a soft high call, is often used when there are young wolves present, when adult females are in estrus, or as a vocal sign of submission. A variation of the whimper is a vocal call labeled the "social squeak," a high-pitched call sometimes used between adult wolves.

One of the most important uses of communication by wolves is in play activity. From a very young age, postures and vocal sounds are used in distinctive ways to initiate play behavior. For most mammals, play behavior is only found in young animals, but for wolves, even adults engage in such "frivolous" activity. When young animals play, they are in effect learning important lessons about survival, mating, hunting, and other aspects of life as adults. Adult wolves play for other reasons — including the establishment and maintenance of social bonds — but some scientists believe that such behavior may exist simply as an outlet for excess energy and because the intelligence of this predator gives it the opportunity to spend some of its time in non-practical conduct.

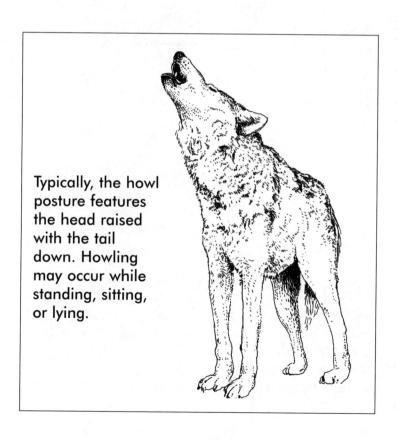

Typically, the howl posture features the head raised with the tail down. Howling may occur while standing, sitting, or lying.

Facial expressions
include movements
of the mouth,
muzzle, eyes,
and ears.

With ears
back, this
expression
conveys fear or
alarm.

Almost the
same expression,
but with the
ears forward,
the communication
here is aggression.

One on one, dominance is communicated by posture. The wolf on top is dominant; the wolf on the bottom expresses submission.

Submission may be communicated with the ears back, the head down, the tail between the legs, or a leg raised to expose the stomach and genitalia.

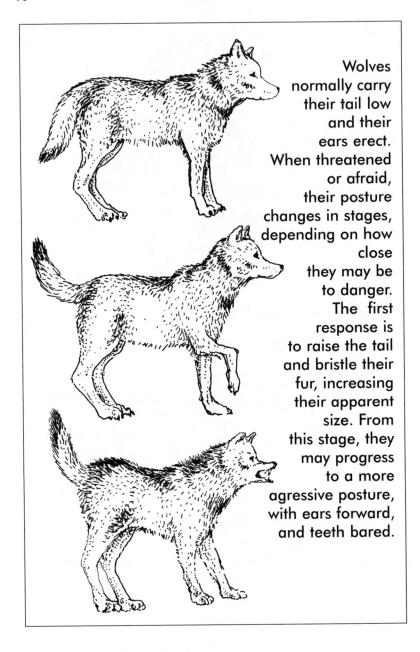

Wolves normally carry their tail low and their ears erect. When threatened or afraid, their posture changes in stages, depending on how close they may be to danger. The first response is to raise the tail and bristle their fur, increasing their apparent size. From this stage, they may progress to a more agressive posture, with ears forward, and teeth bared.

Or, depending on the threat, they may become more submissive or afraid. In this case, the posture includes a lowered tail and ears back. At its most extreme, submission or fear will drive the wolf to make itself smaller, including dropping to the ground with a lowered head.

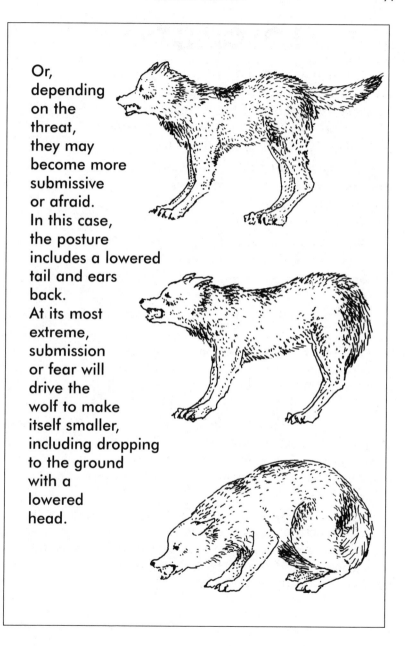

LOCOMOTION

"We rustled through the leaves like wind,
Left shrubs, and trees, and wolves behind;
By night I heard them on the track,
their troop came hard upon our back,
With their long gallop, which can tire
The hound's deep hate, and hunter's fire:
Where'er we flew they followed on,
Nor left us with the morning sun;
Behind I saw them, scarce a rood,
At day-break winding through the wood,
And through the night had heard their feet
Their stealing, rustling step repeat."   — Lord Byron (*Mazeppa*)

An adult wolf with an unhurried pace may have a span of about 24 inches between the front and rear paws, measured by its track. In a hurry, the span may increase to almost 40 inches. A single leap, however, can span an even greater distance, up to sixteen feet according to one observation. The top speed of a running wolf is estimated to be about 43 miles per hour (70 kph). More typically, a normal pace when traveling would be about 5 miles per hour (8 kph). Although the wolf can outrun most of its major prey for short distances — the exception is the caribou — its forte is the prolonged chase, with a marathoner's ability to keep a steady pace for many miles.

Wolves have been known to swim and can maneuver well in a watery environment. In North America, historical observations have recorded wolves swimming across streams, rivers, and lakes. One report from 1926 noted a wolf swimming after a deer more than a mile from the nearest land.

"The wolf also represents a powerful symbol of the character of wild nature. In its wariness of people, the wolf epitomizes our predominant contemporary image of nature: nature as separate from human beings and human beings as divorced from nature. Where we are, there are no wolves; where the wolf lives, there is wilderness."

— Daniel B. Botkin, 1995

At a normal pace, a wolf uses its legs in pairs, one side alternating with the other. But at full speed, the wolf's legs work in tandem the other way, front and rear.

WOLF LOPING

WOLF BOUNDING THROUGH DEEP SNOW

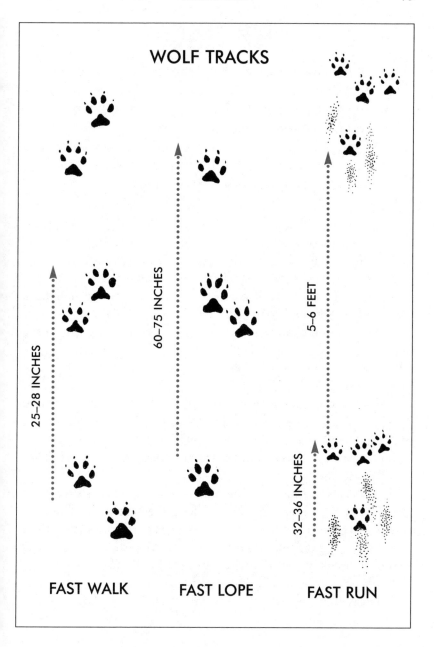

WOLF TRACKS

25–28 INCHES

60–75 INCHES

32–36 INCHES

5–6 FEET

FAST WALK   FAST LOPE   FAST RUN

THE PACK

*"Now this is the Law of the Jungle — as old and as
true as the sky;
And the Wolf that shall keep it may prosper, but the
Wolf that shall break it must die.
As the creeper that girdles the tree-trunk the Law runneth
forward and back — For the strength of the Pack is the
Wolf, and the strength of the Wolf is the Pack."*
— Rudyard Kipling (*The Law of the Jungle*)

In North America, gray wolves normally live and travel in packs. These groups of animals have fluctuating numbers; packs may include more than a dozen animals but typically vary between a few and a dozen, with about six being the average. In rare cases, observers have noted wolf packs with twenty or more members. One wolf pack from Alaska reportedly had thirty-six members.

Packs are often comprised of related animals, the offspring of the dominant pair, referred to as the alpha pair. Pack members may be evenly divided by sex — half male, half female — or have an uneven ratio in either direction.

Red wolves, unlike gray wolves, are less likely to live in packs. The primary social structure of the red wolf is a mated pair, who live and hunt together in their designated territory. However, red wolves do on occasion form packs, but these packs are typically small in size and may be only seasonal.

Gray wolves in packs use communal dens and resting sites, hunt together, and work as a group to defend their territory. The pack system improves the efficiency of hunting for the wolves' primary food source — herd animals that are larger than themselves — and is the predominate reason why this social structure has evolved. Other species of mammals that are predators and prey upon animals larger than themselves — hyenas, jackals, and African hunting dogs, for example — also often live in pack societies. Although hunting success may be the major reason why wolves have evolved to live in packs, the size of the pack does not necessarily relate to the number or size of the prey animals in their territory. Average pack sizes are the same for wolves that hunt deer as for those that hunt moose even though moose are much larger than the deer. And despite the obvious advantage of numbers in comparison to the size of the prey, even the largest of the wolf's traditional prey, the moose, are occasionally attacked and killed by a single wolf.

Biologists speculate that an important factor influencing pack structure and size is a social bond that involves communication and support between pack members. When there are too many members in a pack, this bond becomes unstable and stressful conditions may have negative effects on the health of individuals or the entire group.

Large packs have frequently been observed breaking into smaller groups when hunting. Referred to as pack-splitting, such divisions are usually temporary. The subgroups may remain separated for hours or days, during which the separate units often follow the same paths and hunt in the same areas as when united. Packs may also disband or drift apart during some seasons, especially during denning when young are being born and reared, but return to a single group for the prime winter hunting season. Packs may survive as a unit for many years, but can break up because of aggressiveness between members, disease, lack of prey, or the sexual attraction of wolves in other packs.

LONE WOLVES

"When a wolf goes hunting for his food, we hate him for a destroyer, even though he be starving. When he has sufficient food and kills for the love of sport, we have no language strong enough to condemn the destructive monster...."

— Ernest Thompson Seton, 1925

Although most wolves in North America live in packs, many are temporarily or permanently "lone wolves," living independent lives. Several studies of wolf pack size suggest that of the total wolf population, from 8 to 15 percent may be loners. Low-ranking wolves in packs may be forced to live apart from the family group, but these outcasts are not considered true lone wolves because they stay close to and follow along with their chosen pack. True lone wolves exist completely apart from wolf society.

Why do some wolves live such a solitary existence when their species is driven to live communally? One theory is that such wolves "drop out" of their society because of injury, declining health, or the loss of a mate. Because wolves are so intelligent and exhibit distinctive individual personality traits, it is also possible that lone wolves may just be eccentric compared to other wolves, unable to synchronize with the complex social hierarchy of pack society or just naturally prone to live apart.

Until a few decades ago, all lone wolves were thought to be outcasts from packs. The latest research on wolf society, however, suggests that lone wolves are a regular, recurring part of pack culture, and such animals may come from virtually any part of the social ranking. Even dominant wolves may occasionally set out on their own, but adolescents may be the most common type. Whatever their status, when wolves leave a pack, they act as dispersers of wolf society, expanding territory

FAMOUS LONE WOLVES

Some lone wolves earned reputations as crafty beasts, able to elude the most skillful hunters while they boosted their fearsome carnage of sheep and cattle. In addition to the bounties typically offered for wolves, renegades often attracted premium bounties; the Custer wolf had a $500 bounty on its head.

Old Lefty (Eagle County, Colorado)
Peg Leg
the Phantom Wolf (Fruita, Colorado)
Greenhorn Wolf (Pueblo, Colorado)
The Traveler (west-central Arkansas)
Crip (Texas)
Unaweep Wolf (Unaweep Canyon, Colorado)
Big Foot (DeBeque, Colorado)
Old Whitey (Trinidad, Colorado)
Rags the Digger (Cathedral Bluffs, Colorado)
Old Guy Jumbo
Old Doctor
The King of Currampaw (New Mexico)
The Black Devil
Lobo (northern New Mexico)
Winnipeg Wolf
White Wolf of Pine Ridge
Roosevelt Wolf
White Wolf of Cheyenne
Pryor Creek Wolf (south-central Montana)
Aguila Wolf (Wickenburg, Arizona)
Three Toes (Harding County, South Dakota)
The Custer Wolf (Black Hills, South Dakota)

and founding new ranges almost like human explorers and pioneers.

Lone wolves are a traditional part of wolf lore for human society. For humans, unfortunately, lone wolves have mostly had a negative image, associated with fear of attack, rabies, or threats to agricultural profits. Lone wolves, often referred to as renegade wolves, seem to be more often blamed for raids on livestock than wolf packs. Perhaps because they are not able to effectively compete for their traditional wild food sources, they turn to the next best thing, domesticated animals that are easier to catch and kill. Lone wolves, targeted for their destruction of livestock, often gained added notoriety locally through the use of colorful nicknames.

Some renegade wolves may also have become solitary because their packs were destroyed by wolf hunters. The written history of people and wolves in North America since the mid-1800s is mostly reports and tales of lone wolves. Before that time, reports were mostly about packs.

ANIMAL RELATIONSHIPS

"Beware of false prophets, which come to you in sheep's clothing, but inwardly they are ravening wolves."

— St. Matthew, 15

In most of their natural range in North America, wolves are either the dominant predator or, in the case of bears, operate in non-conflicting ways. Bears and wolves both prey upon large herd animals, but have rarely been known to be threatened by the presence of each other, at least while hunting. On some occasions, bears and wolves may contest the ownership of a carcass or food cache, but this rivalry would not typically result in a physical attack or violence.

With coyotes, on the other hand, wolves are not prone to coexist peaceably. Wolves frequently catch and kill coyotes, often confronting them at a food site. Wolves have also been known to aggressively seek out coyote denning sites and kill coyote cubs. If given the opportunity, coyotes will also attack and kill wolf cubs. A similar relationship exists between wolves and domestic dogs, although numerous reports from European settlers, explorers, and Native Americans indicate that sometimes dogs will run with wolf packs unmolested, especially during breeding seasons.

RAVEN
Corvus corax

Many wildlife observers have noted a stronger symbiotic relationship between wolves and ravens. These large birds are scavengers and benefit from the frequent kills created by wolves. The wolves, in turn, may benefit from the ravens when scavenging for food, as the birds may be more effective at locating carcasses from the air.

HOME TURF

"I have learned of wolves whose master trait was wisdom. I have known of wolves whose animating force was the spirit of adventure." — Ernest Thompson Seton, 1937

The home range of wolves in North America in modern times may not be as typical of the behavior of wolves in past centuries, when they were in greater number and humans were less prevalent. At the extreme, wolves may include areas from 50 square miles to 5,000 square miles, such as in Mount McKinley National Park. Wolves that live in territory populated by migrating prey animals, such as the caribou, may move with a traveling herd up to 100 miles from their normal territory.

Wolves generally mark and keep a consistent territory, especially when their territory is next to or near the territory of other packs. The boundaries are marked with urine, with packs constantly maintaining this special marking during their movements throughout the territory. The objects that are chosen as scent markers are usually physically distinct, such as rocks or trees. When wolves come into contact with human artifacts such as roads or fences, they will often use them as convenient marking spots.

Some wildlife observers believe that prey animals such as deer may respond to hunting pressure from wolf packs by identifying and moving into territory that lies between competing wolf packs. Such "no man's land" adds a measure of protection from attack; the density of prey animals in between wolf packs is often greater than inside the marked territory.

REPRODUCTION

"The dogs of the American aborigines have pointed ears and a drooping tail, constituting a unique species. ... The Indians must have domesticated these dogs long before the [white Spanish] discovery, and old Indians assured me that they had heard their forebearers relate how they had tamed the wolves. The wolves will follow bitches in heat and breed bastard dogs. I had occasion to observe this myself."
— Duke of Württemberg, 1822–1824

Female wolves become sexually mature during their second year but most males do not become sexually mature until their third year. In captivity, wolves may begin breeding much earlier, as young as nine months.

Wolf packs generally confine breeding to a single adult pair, the alpha male and alpha female, but this is not a rigid rule of pack society. Exceptions may occur that allow additional subordinate females within a pack to mate, most likely related to environmental conditions that favor a rapid increase in the size of a pack. A dominant female may not always choose a dominant male with which to mate, especially when there is a high amount of aggression between closely matched males, resulting in successful mating by subordinate males. At other times, subordinate males may also engage in "sneak copulations" when out of sight of dominant males. This behavior may be critically important for the genetic diversity of a wolf population, both in physical characteristics and temperament, adding to the overall adaptability of the population to changing environmental conditions.

A female will be biologically receptive for a few days to a week, a period referred to as estrus. During estrus the female will court and accept a male, but not before. Biologists have reported, however, that female wolves may gradually go into heat, developing signs of estrus up to several weeks before they are sexually receptive.

Unlike many other pack animals, wolves usually maintain the pack social structure during the mating process, even though some aggression and fighting between males and females may be involved. Both the alpha male and the alpha female will actively

ONE DAY OLD

SIX WEEKS OLD

discourage mating between pack members other than themselves.
Lone wolves may travel long distances in search of a mate and
female wolves are assertive in their pursuit of potential males. As
with many predators, the female wolf will usually prefer and choose
the largest, strongest male. Lone male or female wolves have been
observed courting domestic dogs during mating periods.

Reproduction in wolves is similar to that of domestic dogs,
with the male mounting the female from the rear. The two animals are locked together during copulation. Two unique biological characteristics are involved in this wolf-to-wolf "tie." The
base of the penis, known as the bulbus glandis in the wolf, swells
after copulation is initiated. In the female, this swelling triggers a
corresponding constriction of sphincter muscles around the vagina,

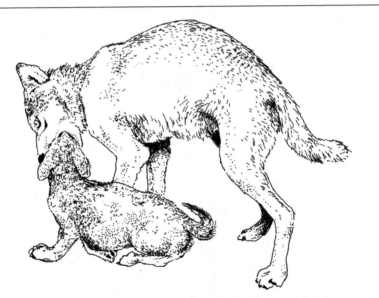

**Young wolves are weaned with partially digested food
regurgitated by their parents or other adult wolves.**

clamping down on the swollen penis. The wolf pair may be locked together for several minutes, up to half an hour, a vulnerable period which wolf hunters have in the past exploited to kill or capture animals. Some wolf experts believe, however, that unlike domesticated dogs, copulating wolves can separate if threatened. The male wolf is thought to begin ejaculating when he is first locked into the female; the ejaculation continues throughout the tie.

Most alpha pairs mate exclusively with one another, but numerous exceptions have been noted. A female wolf may accept a new alpha male; an alpha male may accept different females. The mating period is January to April with the earliest mating periods found for wolves living in the southernmost areas; the latest periods correspond with the northernmost ranges. The gestation period is about 63 days but can vary by up to four days. Coyotes also have a gestation period of 63 days. The gestation period for domestic dogs may vary by breed but it averages 63 days.

Through an unknown biological mechanism, the size of each litter is related to the size of the wolf population in the local area, the amount of prey available, and other environmental stresses. If a wolf pack is large, for instance, litter sizes are most likely to be small; when a pack is small in size, litter sizes are most likely to be large. The size of neighboring packs may also influence litter size. At the extreme, some wolf packs may not reproduce in a given season. Observers have noted that this is most likely to occur during periods of food shortages. Litters range in size from three to 12 young, with six being an average. As few as one pup may be born in a litter, and at least one litter of 14 pups has been observed.

As the pups are born, mother wolves use their teeth to break through the amniotic sac and their tongue to strip it off the newborn. The mother severs the umbilical cord with her teeth and eats this, the amniotic sac, and the afterbirth. During the first few weeks in the den, the mother wolf or other adults may stimulate the young to urinate and defecate by licking their stomachs and anal areas.

Wolf pups are born blind and deaf. Their eyes open within the first two weeks although the young animals may not be able to distinguish most visual images at the beginning. The ears of young wolves are limp and floppy, becoming erect and movable beginning about the fourth week. Also about the fourth week, wolf pups may utter their first howls. Baby wolves are born without teeth, but a limited set of milk teeth emerge beginning in their second week of life. Milk teeth include incisors, canines, premolars, and molars, but none of these are permanent. The milk teeth of young wolves are lost beginning about sixteen weeks, replaced by a new set that has the characteristics necessary for tearing and ripping meat.

Wolf pups may begin emerging from their dens by the end of their third week, but they are still dependent on the mother wolf and the protection of the den for another few weeks, until they are weaned and more capable of moving around. Mother wolves usually begin weaning their young during the fifth week after birth. Weaning is accomplished by introducing the pups to regurgitated food, a food supply that may come from both parents and other adult members of the pack. Pups can stimulate the regurgitation by licking or nipping at the adults' mouths and muzzles, but it is not always necessary.

Physical growth for wolves is mostly over by the end of their first year. They may gain more weight in future months and after the first year, but the primary indicator of adult physical status — the length of their leg bones — has become permanent.

DENNING

*"They always burrow under-ground to bring forth their
young; and though it is natural to suppose them very fierce
at those times, yet I have frequently seen the Indians go to
their dens, and take out the young ones and play with them.
I never knew a Northern Indian hurt one of them: on the
contrary, they always put them carefully into the den again;
and I have sometimes seen them paint the faces of the
young Wolves with vermillion, or red ochre."*
— Samuel Hearne, 1769–1772

Wolves do not normally use dens except when giving birth and
raising young. Dens are often created from scratch by pregnant females, who begin digging excavations or burrows a month or
more before birth begins. Den sites are often chosen for their soft or
sandy soil, making digging easier. Dens may also be appropriated
from existing natural cavities or those made by bears, foxes, or other
animals. Caves, rotten logs, spaces created by exposed tree roots,
and even beaver homes are also used for wolf dens. It is believed
that wolves do not, however, attack or drive off beavers or other
animals in order to expropriate their dwellings, but choose abandoned sites. In some parts of their range, wolves may use the same
den for many years and through more than one generation.

Burrows dug by wolves are rarely more than one to two feet in
diameter, but can extend up to fourteen feet in length, connecting
to a birthing chamber that may be wider than the tunnel. Some wolf
dens have more than one entrance tunnel. Den sites are typically
close to natural supplies of water such as creeks or lakes, an important resource for nursing mothers.

Except for the mother wolf, adult wolves rest on the open ground,
although they often select bedding sites protected by stands of
brush or timber. Denning sites have been observed being used

repeatedly from year to year by the same wolf packs, but some wolves use more than one denning site in the same year. A pack has been observed moving at least four times in the same season, carrying the pups to the new dens every few weeks. When more than one wolf in a pack has a litter at the same time, more than one den may be used, and there have been reports of more than one litter sharing the same den at the same time.

Pups begin exploring outside of their dens at about four weeks of age but may not move around outside actively until they are six to eight weeks old. Pups and their mothers begin abandoning dens for an outdoor existence at about eight weeks after birth. Most litters have abandoned their dens by the tenth week. At this point, some observers have noted that wolves may use other open areas as resting sites until the young wolves are able to travel with the pack and participate in hunts, usually by the fall or winter following their birth. These resting sites were dubbed "rendezvous sites" by Paul Joslin, one of the first researchers to study this unique period in wolf development.

HUNTING

"Domesticated animals, unprotected, cannot resist the persevering attacks of wolves, urged on as they are by their appetites, and conducting their warfare with all the skill of instinct, sharpened often by famine. The deer and the antelope are compelled frequently to shelter themselves from the attacks of these animals, under the strong protection of buffaloes, and you sometimes see herds of buffaloes and antelopes mingled and grazing together."

— Edwin Bryant, 1885

Wolves in North America are typically active in the evening and night in the summer season. In the winter, hunting is also common during the daylight hours, and wolves may hunt during either the day or night. The preference is linked to the activities of the herd animals being hunted. These herd mammals may also go through seasonal movements within the home range of a wolf pack, influencing how far wolves must travel from their resting sites to find food. Depending on the location and season, hunting wolves may travel from a few miles to 40 miles in a day.

Hunting travel by wolves may involve a direct route, a straight path from where they began to a hunting site. At times, wolves may travel in widely erratic directions, searching for food by random discovery. During the denning season, however, observers have noted that wolves will invariably take more direct paths, especially when they are carrying food back to the den. The paths that wolves use within their territories may be well-defined and followed consistently. These well-used paths may have been developed in response to the equally consistent habits of the local prey animals. In some parts of their range, such paths are permanent, well-established routes that vary little over many generations.

Wolves have the ability to work their way through deep layers of snow; but often packs will use a single line of file to take advantage of the trail created by the lead wolf, a method that saves considerable energy for the pack. Numerous hunters, trackers, and wolf researchers, however, have noted that in snowy conditions, wolves frequently take paths with the least resistance from snow. This includes frozen lakes and streams, wind-blown areas, shorelines, roadways, and paths created by other animals, skiers, and snowmobiles.

Routes favored by wolves include well-established trails — sometimes referred to as runways — that may be used for many generations. In some wolf territories, observers have mapped networks of regular wolf trails that form interconnecting circuits. Some of these travel systems also overlap with the circuits of neighboring packs; in a few cases, the overlaps may include some trails shared by more than one pack. Circuits that have been measured are from about thirty to almost ninety miles in length. Although these runways may be used continually and repetitively, the wolves using them do

Muskoxen have developed a unique group defense against wolves. The males form a defensive circle, with their horns facing out. The defense may break down, however, if attacking wolves succeed in producing confusion among their prey, causing the muskoxen to abandon the group and flee, leaving individual animals less protected.

"The day before yesterday one of my neighbors told me that he had caught a wolf. He wanted to turn the dogs loose on him and invited me to watch the fight. In company with others we immediately set out with four dogs. The pit or trap built of tree trunks was a mile away from human habitations. Through gaps between the logs we could see the beast of prey lying quietly on the floor of his cage. By means of wooden hooks the men pulled out his hind legs and cut the tendons, a procedure that could scarcely be accomplished because of the constant attempts of the dogs to attack him. Then the cover was lifted and immediately all the dogs fell upon the prisoner. Disregarding his serious injuries he easily forced his way from the trap and only then really began to defend himself. It was a full-grown male. The dogs were his equals in size and all were of a breed called butcher's cur. The wolf tried to escape, but since the dogs prevented him from doing this he squatted from time to time on his mutilated hindquarters and in a sitting position bit to the right and left so that even the bravest of his opponents emitted many a howl of pain. By his defensive tactics he tired the dogs so much that one after another ran to a neighboring ditch, cooled off by bathing in it, and then returned to resume the fight. Although my companions insisted that this cruel game was necessary to train their dogs, the courageous defense of the helpless beast finally aroused the sympathy of everyone and the torture was brought to an end by a well-aimed blow to his head."

— Gottfried Duden
Report on a Journey to the Western States of North America and a Stay of Several Years Along the Missouri, 1825

not follow a predictable schedule or route from one circuit to the next.

Wolves and wolf packs have evolved to become effective at hunting and killing prey animals that are larger than themselves. In fact, the pack itself is likely a biological adaptation to allow such predators to be able to utilize large herd animals as a food source. Most herd animals in North America are not only larger than wolves, but they can run faster — some can run farther — and are usually equipped with horns or antlers that are effective defensive weapons. Hooves may also inflict damaging and even deadly blows during attacks, and the hair and hides of these large prey are thick and tough, a difficult barrier against the teeth of predators.

That wolves can thrive amidst these challenges is a mark of their intelligence and hunting skills. Only human intervention has had any effect at decreasing wolf populations. The herd animals, however, also thrive, because they have evolved at the same time to balance the power of their predators. If the prey animals were not able to offset the predation by wolves, they would become extinct; if the wolves were not able to offset the defenses of the prey animals, they would either become extinct or be forced to adapt to prey upon something else.

Although wolves have developed the necessary power and skill to use herd animals as their main food supply, the balance of power is enough that during most hunts, wolves deliberately select individual animals that give the wolves an edge. The selection process targets prey animals that are sick, injured, old, weak, or immature, all characteristics that deprive the animal of its maximum capability at evading capture or defending itself.

Wolf senses are acutely capable of performing this selection. Sight, sound, and smell may all be used to pick out the weakest members of a herd. Instinct is important in this process, but it is most likely the intelligence and learned behavior of the wolves that gives them the decision-making power to choose the right target.

PREDATOR/PREY SIZE COMPARISON

AS A FOOD SOURCE

Wolves have been a source of food in North America, but they have not been a major or consistent part of any culture's diet. Some Indian tribes ate the meat if and when a wolf was killed; others would not eat the animal under any circumstances. Early settlers and explorers occasionally resorted to eating wolf, including Lewis and Clark and Fremont during their expeditions. Some Indians in the Canadian territories were reported to use wolf fat in the making of pemmican, a traditional staple of native cultures in North America, and a few tribes actively bred wolves in captivity as a source of meat.

Younger wolves, for example, may not exhibit the same hunting patterns as more mature wolves, with the younger wolves more likely to target the first animal they see.

Many reports over the years have suggested that wolves have group hunting techniques that utilize coordinated strategies to stalk, surround, or ambush prey. David Mech, among other experts, however, believes that there is too little evidence to make this more than a theory. His observations instead point to a simpler and more direct hunting practice, individual wolves or packs traveling until they encounter an animal they can catch and eat. This type of random searching is also common with other types of predators, from insects to marine mammals. Heightened powers of sense — sight, smell, hearing — may be useful in targeting a specific animal or pinpointing the location of an animal or a herd, but being in the right area to find the animals in the first place involves some chance.

After detecting prey, wolves exhibit specific kinds of stalking behavior. They may attempt to get as close to the prey as possible through stealthy maneuvers, quietly approaching with the wind in their faces, reducing the chance that the prey will be alerted to their presence through smell. This type of stalking may allow wolves to get within 100 feet before launching an attack and occasionally, observers have seen wolves sneak within much closer distances before detection.

Herd animals typically run away from wolves after they have been spotted. Some, however — moose, for example — will stand and confront approaching wolves, at least for a few minutes. Some wolf biologists believe that wolves — as well as some other species of predators — may not be stimulated to attack their prey unless the prey is moving. Running would thus be a catalyst that triggers the wolf to pursue the prey. Evidence from observers supports this theory; numerous wolf-prey encounters have been noted where the wolves failed to attack the prey while they remain still, even if there was only a single prey animal present and the wolves were hunting in a pack.

The wolves may also be better suited to killing their prey if it is running away, allowing them to slash and grab at unprotected body parts. When confronted by a horned or antlered animal physically much larger than themselves, they would face a greater risk of injury or death from the animal's defenses.

When chasing herd animals, wolves generally are only successful at making a kill if they catch an animal within the first half-mile. Although wolf chases have been observed lasting up to five miles, most chases after the first half-mile are to the advantage of the prey. Moose, elk, caribou, deer, and Dall sheep are among the prey animals that have been observed outrunning wolves. Typically, when these animals have achieved a safe distance, they will stop running and wait to see if their pursuers continue the chase before running again, thereby saving energy.

Herd animals also exhibit an ability to discount the presence of

While hunting, wolves typically follow a leader. In snow, maintaining a single file helps conserve energy, with the first wolf making a path for the others.

wolves if the wolves are not actively hunting. Individual wolves and wolf packs have been observed moving through and near herds of prey without triggering defensive postures or a rush to escape. One theory explaining this prey behavior is that features of approaching wolves — the position of the tail, ears, or general posture — may be recognizable to the prey as threatening or benign.

Caribou herds are also often deliberately stampeded by wolves in order to target individual prey. Caribou can outrun wolves if healthy and mature but while running away from wolves, the herd may outdistance weak, injured, or juvenile members. These slower runners are most likely to become the final target of the wolf attack. Within a large caribou herd, one or more wolves may also successively chase smaller groups until a vulnerable animal is selected.

Wolves in North America have also been observed using an ambush technique to catch their prey. This ambushing is mostly found where wolves hunt caribou. A caribou ambush may involve one or more wolves circling around a traveling herd and waiting for the herd to approach. In some of these cases, they hide uphill from the caribou and rush or pounce on their prey when the distance has narrowed. A few observers have seen a more sophisticated version of this ambush activity in which part of a pack may drive caribou toward an ambush site where the rest of the pack hides in anticipation.

Overall, wolves fail to capture and kill their prey more often then they succeed. One specific study of the hunting success of wolves is based on their predation on moose. For this prey, David Mech has concluded that wolves are successful about 8 to 10 percent of the time after they have begun an attack. A similar or even smaller rate is likely to apply to the other major herd animals wolves hunt in North America. Some studies have shown that most of the herd animals killed by wolves are young — from newborn to less than one year old — or past their prime. Calculations of this predatory behavior are similar for moose, caribou, bighorn sheep, Dall sheep, muskox, bison, and deer. The average age of prey may vary from summer to winter, but the overall statistics remain fairly constant. The sex of the prey animal does not seem to be a major factor in their selection by hunting wolves.

Herd animals are also targeted by wolves because of their physical condition. Weaker animals may not be able to keep up with the herd, making them more vulnerable to attack, and they are also less able to defend themselves when attacked. Some studies of wolf prey have shown that certain diseases may be a contributing factor to the loss of strength. Diseases which have been identified as contributing to prey mortality include malnutrition, tapeworm, and "lumpy jaw" or actinomycosis (in moose and Dall sheep). Previously broken bones or wounds are also commonly found in herd animals preyed upon by wolves.

In contrast, in cases where wolves have attacked domesticated animals, the wolves are thought to be much less careful about their targets. They select the largest and healthiest animals more often than when preying on wild animals. Biologists believe this is likely to be from the lack of defensive instincts in the domestic beasts, where sensing, alarm, and flight behavior has been lost through breeding.

The large herd animals that are targeted as prey are brought down by one or more wolves, the large canine teeth used for grabbing and leverage. Most prey are attacked at the hindquarters, head, or neck. The smallest prey — deer and caribou — are most often grabbed near the front; moose are most often grabbed near the rear.

It has long been stated in popular literature that wolves disable running herd animals by slashing the tendons in the rear legs, "hamstringing" their prey. Among the major wolf biologists in North America in the modern era, however, none have ever found evidence that wolves have used this method on wild animals. However such a myth was started, the reality is that such action is avoided by wolves because of the lethal force represented by the rear hooves of their prey. A blow from this limb from such a large animal can cripple or kill the smaller wolf. Hamstringing might be used by some wolves when attacking non-wild animals such as cattle or sheep, because these creatures may have lost some of their instinctive abilities to defend themselves with their hooves.

Wolves do not show a clear preference for which part of a prey animal they will eat first, although some observers believe they are most likely to start with whatever part has already been ripped open during an attack, often the hindquarters. Another favored dining site is the stomach cavity, ripped open to expose the internal organs. The internal organs are also exposed by gnawing through the rib cage.

Examination of carcass remains after wolf kills shows that if not interrupted or distracted, wolves will eat virtually all of the body of their prey. Parts that may be left behind include pieces of the hide and some bones, most notably the skull, lower jaw, and spine.

Fragments of other bones may also be discarded, chips and shards created when wolves crunch through limbs to get to the bone marrow.

Most of the time, wolves are thorough in their eating activity. Studies of carcasses killed and eaten by wolves show that most of the time — two-thirds to three quarters of the kills examined — they will consume at least 75 percent of the animals' bodies. Some studies of wolf attacks on domesticated animals — sheep and cattle — show that they are much less thorough with this type of food source. Only 30 percent or less of these prey were consumed entirely.

Small animals such as mice, beaver, and ground squirrels — as well as dogs and cats — are usually completely consumed and the smallest ones eaten whole.

Once wolves have made a kill, they may remain in one location for one or more days, depending on how long it takes them to consume the animal. In between feeding periods, the pack may rest close to the carcass or travel to a sheltered area in the vicinity. Wolf packs have been observed killing and eating adult moose and caribou with the feeding process taking two or more days before the animal was completely consumed. Smaller prey animals — adult deer or juveniles of all species — may be completely consumed within a few hours and in some cases, the wolves may move on to make another kill in the same day.

Under extreme conditions, wolves may be able to go long periods without food, up to two weeks or more by some estimates. During such periods, however, wolves may find small, insignificant sources of food such as plant material or leftover bones or hide from former kills. Wolves in most areas are also prone to catch and eat numerous small animals such as rodents, birds, and reptiles, but even though they may consume large numbers of such animals, the overall percentage by weight of their food intake usually remains well less than half of their total diet.

Where the prey animals are migratory, such as the caribou, wolf packs may travel more extensively, keeping pace with their food supply. Some biologists believe this makes the wolf a migratory animal itself. In any case, such wolf packs still remain within a territory that is established as their own. Within established territories, some wolf packs follow distinctive seasonal migrations of their own, moving down to lower elevations in the snowiest months, and up to the highest elevations when the weather is milder. On the great plains during the era of the buffalo, wolves may have also had more extensive travel habits than in modern times.

WOLF PREY

Caribou
Rangifer tarandus

RANGE

VITAL STATISTICS

NAME	Caribou, referred to as Reindeer when domesticated Scientific name: *Rangifer tarandus*
DESCRIPTION	Both sexes antlered; antlers sweeping with projecting tines; brown to gray, dark and light shades; belly, inside of legs, and rear paler; winter coat lighter; distinctive mane of longer hair on underside of neck; large, elongated muzzle; estimated population 3 million

HEAD+BODY LENGTH	47–87 " 120–220 cm	**TAIL LENGTH**	3–8 " 7–21 cm
WEIGHT	132–700 lbs 60–318 kg	**HEIGHT AT SHOULDER**	34–55 " 87–140 cm

HOME RANGE	Northern Idaho and Washington, British Columbia, northern Alaska, northern Canada
HABITAT	Tundra; conifer forests
FOOD	Shrubs, lichens, twigs, ground plants, conifer leaves
BREEDING	Birth in May and June; gestation period 227–229 days; single births; sexually mature 17 to 41 months
HABITS	Mostly diurnal; fastest running speed 35–50 miles/hour (60–80 km/hr); poor eyesight; acute sense of smell; seasonal migrations between summer and winter ranges; travels in large, dense herds during migrations; average longevity 4.5 years; can live more than 15 years

Elk
Cervus elaphus

RANGE

VITAL STATISTICS

NAME	Elk, also known as wapiti and red deer Scientific name: *Cervus elaphus*
DESCRIPTION	Antlers unusually large and branched with a secondary set of tines between the main antlers; shades of brown, lighter color on belly and rear; distincitive longer hair forms mane

HEAD+BODY LENGTH	65–104 " 165–265 cm	**TAIL LENGTH**	4–11 " 10–27 cm
WEIGHT	165–750 " 75–340 kg	**HEIGHT AT SHOULDER**	30–59 " 75–150 cm

HOME RANGE	California, Rocky Mountains, parts of Canada
HABITAT	Conifer forests, hardwood forests, grasslands, chaparral
FOOD	Grasses, woody plants, broadleaf plants, shrubbery, conifer leaves
BREEDING	Birthing late spring; gestation period 247–265 days; single calves; sexually mature after 2 years
HABITS	Diurnal; in some parts of range may migrate from summer to winter habitats; lives in herds of 4–400, larger groups may number 1,000; longevity 5–10 years; may live for more than 20 years

Moose
Alces alces

RANGE

VITAL STATISTICS

NAME	Moose, also called elk in Europe Scientific name: *Alces alces*		
DESCRIPTION	Large, flattened antlers; largest member of the deer family; color black to brown, sometimes reddish, lighter in color on belly and legs; seasonal variation: darker in winter, lighter in summer; large muzzle with an overhanging lip; large, loose flap of skin on underside of neck		
HEAD+BODY LENGTH	94–122 " 240–310 cm	**TAIL LENGTH**	2–5 " 5–12 cm
WEIGHT	441–1820 lbs 200–825 kg	**HEIGHT AT SHOULDER**	55–93 lbs 140–235 cm
HOME RANGE	Canada, Alaska, upper parts of Great Lakes states, upper parts of New England, Rocky Mountains		
HABITAT	Wooded areas, favors damp ground with shrubs, poplar, and willow		
FOOD	Shrubbery, greenery, twigs, bark, ground plants, aquatic plants and roots		
BREEDING	Mates in fall; birthing in spring months; gestation period 226–264 days; one calf per litter; twins common; sexually mature at 2 years		
HABITS	Diurnal; mostly solitary; can run up to 35 miles/hour (56 km/h); poor vision; senses of smell and hearing acute; moves between summer and winter ranges up to 110 miles (179 km); longevity up to 27 years		

Bison
Bison bison

RANGE

VITAL STATISTICS

NAME	Bison, also called buffalo Scientific name: *Bison bison*
DESCRIPTION	Short horns that curve in and forward, horns on both sexes, smaller horns on female; color various shades of brown, may be reddish; longer hair on shoulders and under neck; pelt longer and shaggier in winter; short, broad head; distinctive hump over shoulders; short legs; distinctive beard

HEAD+BODY LENGTH	83–138 " 210–350 cm	**TAIL LENGTH**	12–24 " 30–60 cm
WEIGHT	772–2200 lbs 350–1000 kg	**HEIGHT AT SHOULDER**	60–80 " 150–200 cm

HOME RANGE	Isolated herds in parks and ranches in western U.S. and Canada. For original range, see page 15
HABITAT	Grasslands, plains
FOOD	Ground cover, grasses
BREEDING	Birthing in spring months; gestation period 285 days; single calf; sexual maturity 2–4 years
HABITS	Mostly diurnal; lives and travels in family herds, may gather in larger herds numbering in the thousands; poor eyesight; senses of hearing and smell acute; top running speed 35 miles/hour (60 km/h); traditional seasonal migrations now limited by lack of range; moves from higher to lower elevations in winter; longevity more than 20 years

Muskox
Ovibos moschatus

RANGE

VITAL STATISTICS

NAME	Muskox Scientific name: *Ovibos moschatus*		
DESCRIPTION	Large horns curve down and up, extending from bony plate on top of head, horns on both sexes; color brown to dark brown, lighter color on back and legs; distinctive coat of long shaggy hair, can reach to the ground; small hump on shoulders; short legs; males much larger than females		
HEAD+BODY LENGTH	75–90 " 190–230 cm	TAIL LENGTH	3–4 " 9–10 cm
WEIGHT	500–900 lbs 225–405 kg	HEIGHT AT SHOULDER	36–60 " 91–152 cm
HOME RANGE	Northern Canada, northern Alaska, Greenland		
HABITAT	Arctic tundra, prefers damp areas in summer months		
FOOD	Grasses, sedges, broadleafed plants, berries, willow, woody plants		
BREEDING	Birthing mid-April to mid-June; gestation period 8-9 months; single calves, sexually mature 2–5 years		
HABITS	Senses of hearing and eyesight acute; lives in groups of ten or more, may form large herds; herds form distincitve defensive lines against wolves; top speed 25 miles/hour (40 km/h); longevity up to 24 years		

White-tailed Deer
Odocoileus virginianus

Mule Deer
Odocoileus hemionus

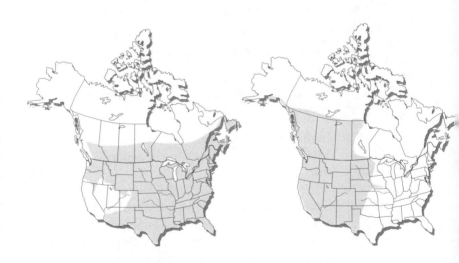

RANGE

VITAL STATISTICS

NAME	Deer, also called white-tailed deer, mule deer Scientific name: *Odocoileus virginianus, O. hemionus*
DESCRIPTION	Color brown, brownish-gray, gray, reddish in winter, lighter colors on belly and inside legs. White-tailed: antlers have one beam with branching; tail brown on top, white on sides and underneath; ear one-half length of head. Mule: antlers branch into two sections; tail white or black on top with black tip; ear two-thirds or more length of head

HEAD+BODY LENGTH	33–83 " 85–210 cm	**TAIL LENGTH**	4–14 " 10–35 cm
WEIGHT	75–400 lbs 34–181 kg	**HEIGHT AT SHOULDER**	22–43 " 55–110 cm

HOME RANGE	White-tailed: U.S. and Canada except for southwest. Mule: western U.S., western Canada
HABITAT	White-tailed: forests, swamps, open areas Mule: coniferous forests, chaparral, grasslands
FOOD	Grasses, weeds, mushrooms, twigs, shrubbery, nuts, lichens, orchards, garden and farm crops
BREEDING	Birthing April-September; gestation period 195–212 days; single fawns, twins and higher multiple births common; sexually mature 1–2 years
HABITS	Diurnal; often live in family groups, may form larger herds in winter; top speed 40 miles/hour (64 km/h); longevity up to 20 years

Dall Sheep
Ovis dalli

Mountain Goat
Oreamnos americanus

Bighorn Sheep
Ovis canadensis

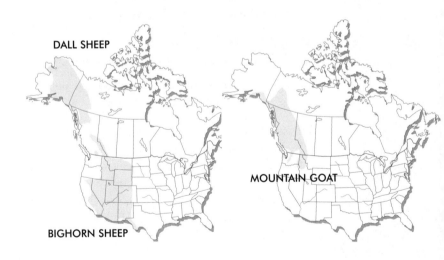

DALL SHEEP

BIGHORN SHEEP

MOUNTAIN GOAT

RANGE

VITAL STATISTICS

NAME	Dall Sheep, Bighorn Sheep, Mountain Goat Scientific names: *Ovis dalli, O. canadensis, Oreamnos americanus*
DESCRIPTION	Dall and bighorn sheep: massive horns spiraling down and forward; color white or gray to black, white or cream rump patch, lighter color on belly; males larger than females. Mountain goat: short black horns curve back; color white or yellowish; fur long and shaggy; long hair under chin forms beard

HEAD+BODY LENGTH	Sheep: 52–60 " Goats: 48–70 "	**TAIL LENGTH**	Sheep: 3–5 " Goats: 3–8 "
WEIGHT	Sheep: 125–200 lbs Goats: 100–300 lbs	**HEIGHT AT SHOULDER**	Sheep: 33–42 " Goats: 36–42 "

HOME RANGE	Dall: Alaska and northwestern Canada. Bighorn: southwestern Canada south to Mexico. Mountain goat: western Canada, southeastern Alaska, northern Idaho and Montana
HABITAT	Sheep: high, rough slopes in mountainous terrain. Mountain goat: at or above timberline.
FOOD	Grasses, sedges, broadleafed plants, shrubbery, woody plants, mosses, lichens
BREEDING	Gestation period 6 months; single offspring; sexually mature 2.5 years
HABITS	Sheep: diurnal; lives in herds, usually less than 12; longevity about 15 years. Goats: diurnal; lives in small herds; longevity about 12 years

FOOD SOURCES

"I now suspect that just as a deer herd lives in mortal fear of its wolves, so does a mountain live in mortal fear of its deer. And perhaps with better cause, for while a buck pulled down by wolves can be replaced in two or three years, a range pulled down by too many deer may fail of replacement in as many decades."

— Aldo Leopold, 1949

In most areas of their range, the gray wolf diet is mostly large mammals such as elk and deer. In the red wolf range, the white-tailed deer is the only large herd animal that is a regular part of the diet. Large herd animals may comprise 75 percent or more of the wolves' food supply, depending on the season. In warm seasons, the widest variety in diet may occur, with smaller mammals, reptiles, fish, and birds added to the menu.

The large animal diet: moose, caribou, elk, bison, mule deer, sitka deer, white-tailed deer, pronghorn antelope, bighorn sheep, mountain goat, Dall sheep, and muskox.

The small animal diet: marmots, ground squirrels, tundra voles, singing voles, beavers, pocket gophers, cotton rats, deer mice, wood rats, kangaroo rats, arctic hares, lemmings, ptarmigans, grouse, snowshoe hares, mice, ducks, geese, porcupines, raccoons, muskrats, turkeys, and woodchucks.

Other food that may be part of the wolf diet includes mollusks, birds' eggs, fish, reptiles (snakes, turtles, lizards, etc.), fruit and berries, and insects. The diet of red wolves may also include cactus fruit. Wolves may also eat other wolves, although it is not believed that one wolf would attack and kill another wolf just to get a meal. Rather, the carcass of a dead wolf may be utilized as food if the circumstances are appropriate. Cattle, horses, and sheep are the domesticated livestock most likely to fall prey to wolves in modern times, but in previous eras pigs were also a major target. Domesticate dogs and cats may also be attacked and eaten.

Fruit that may be an occasional part of the wolf diet includes berries, plums, apples, cherries, and others. In Russia, it has been reported that wild wolves have even eaten watermelons in the field. Vegetation may not comprise more than a few percent of the total diet of wolves, but it is also sometimes eaten for more than its nutritional value. Grasses and other plants are thought to be eaten at times to aid digestion or fight parasites.

In practice, wolves usually do not make a kill of a large mammal every day. They may go several days or even weeks between kills, although this may be because of poor hunting success rather than a lack of interest. Especially with their favored large prey, wolves on the hunt do not catch a meal every time they try and most of the prey they select are young, newborn or less than one year old. In numbers, an individual wolf will catch, kill, and consume many more small mammals — rabbits, mice, and ground squirrels — than large mammals such as elk. The largest percentage of food eaten over time, however, will almost always consist of protein from large animals than that of small mammals. In one study of wolves in northern Alaska, for instance, the animals studied ate almost four times as many arctic ground squirrels as caribou, their preferred prey, but the numbers did not add up to the total quantity of meat provided by the caribou.

Several studies have analyzed wolf diets in terms of daily intake. Although there may be great variation from day to day in how much food a wolf consumes — or even if it eats at all — an individual wolf in the wild may consume from 6–15 pounds (2.7–6.7 kg) of meat per day, an average of 2–3 ounces per pound of wolf (0.10–0.19 kg/kg) per day. Wolves require a minimum of about 2.5 pounds (1.5 kg) of meat per day to remain healthy. An average wolf of 80 pounds (36 kg) requires about 1,450–2,200 calories per day for typical activity. Their average intake in the wild is about 5.5 pounds (3.3 kg).

SMALL ANIMAL MENU

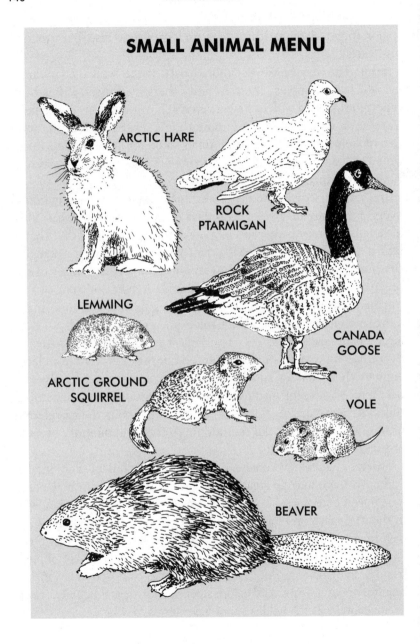

ARCTIC HARE

ROCK PTARMIGAN

CANADA GOOSE

LEMMING

ARCTIC GROUND SQUIRREL

VOLE

BEAVER

LARGE ANIMAL MENU

Tracking wolves in the wild, observers in northern Alberta have recorded that over time, wolves kill about one bison per week. Where wolves feed on moose, over time they consume about 10–14 pounds per day (4.4–6.3 kg/day). Where deer is the main part of the diet, the average is 6–8 pounds per day (2.5–3.6 kg/day).

Wolves are opportunistic when hungry and will often eat carrion or steal food from other predators if given the chance. Reports from both Native Americans and European explorers described wolves scavenging bison that had been killed in large numbers by flood waters and ice. Wolves took advantage of thawing conditions to feast on this bounty. With their largest prey, most wolves do not devour an entire animal at the time it is killed, but feed from it for one or more days until it has been reduced to inedible scraps.

Wolves have been known to bury uneaten food for later use. Burying the food helps to protect it from raids by other predators or scavengers, from foxes to vultures. Caching is not usually very elaborate; the wolves often just partially cover their food with dirt, leaves, or loose ground litter. In the northern parts of its range, extreme cold helps preserve kills and less burying or camouflaging behavior is common.

MORTALITY

"Wolves have always been so great an annoyance that much pains have been taken for their extermination."
— Zadock Thompson, 1853

Although wolves are at the top of their food chain, they are frequently victims of diseases, accidents, and other forces that often lead to death before their maximum biological lifespan. Gray wolves typically live only 5–10 years in the wild. Individual wolves have been known to live for at least 16 years in the wild, but this is an exception. In captivity, wolves may live up to 20 years.

Although wolves are attentive parents, their young are occasionally attacked and killed by bears, cougars, lynx, eagles, wolverines, and other predators. Adult wolves in North America are also occasionally killed by bears, and injuries suffered while chasing prey — particularly from horned animals such as elk and moose — will sometimes result in death. Any injury which reduces a wolf's ability to spot, chase, or kill prey may result in death from starvation. Rival wolf packs may also inflict injury or death during fights over territory or food.

The most vulnerable time for wolves is when they are young. As newborn pups, they may die from malnutrition, disease, or violence. Diseases common to young wolves include distemper, pneumonia, hypothermia, listeriosis, encephalitis, and epilepsy. The mortality rate for wolf pups in the first six months is about 60 percent. From six months to one year of age, the mortality rate is less than 50 percent; mature wolves have an annual mortality rate of about 20 percent.

Parasites which afflict wolves are usually acquired from other wolves. These include tapeworms, fleas, roundworms, heartworms, and mites. Ticks can also transmit disease. The mange mite is responsible for the transmission of mange, a disease which afflicts the skin. Mange results in irregular patches of fur being lost and open sores and scabs caused by scratching to relieve itching. In severe cases wolves may lose all their fur. Older wolves and those previously injured may be susceptible to arthritis. This disease of the joints can disrupt the normal food gathering behavior of a wolf and lead to its death by malnutrition or starvation. Another disease affecting wolves is cancer, with both wild and captive animals observed as victims.

From a human perspective, however, the most striking wolf disease is rabies. Common among many mammals, rabies tends to excite much fear and apprehension in humans — especially when

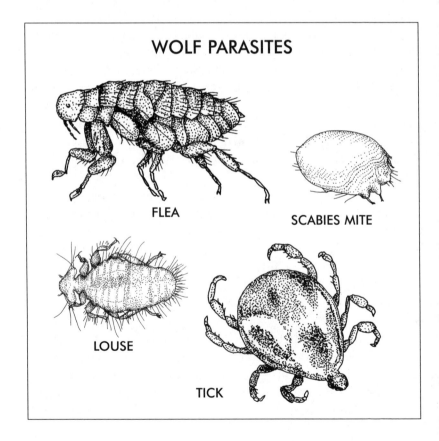

WOLF PARASITES

FLEA

SCABIES MITE

LOUSE

TICK

UNHEALTHY CONDITIONS

Diseases and parasites which affect wolves include ...

tularemia
  (spread by ticks)
hookworms
spiney headed worms
mange mite
  (*Sarcoptes scabei*)
bovine tuberculosis
infectious canine
  hepatitis
trichinosis

hydrophobia
brucellosis
distemper
pneumonia
hypothermia
listeriosis
encephalitis
epilepsy
cancer
arthritis

it appears in dogs and wolves — because animals afflicted with rabies often lost their fear of people, attacking and causing injuries as well as passing on the disease to the victims of their attacks.

As early as 1166 A.D., rabid wolves have been reported in litera-ture. In that year, an afflicted wolf in Wales bit 22 people and most of them died. In North America, reports of rabid wolves abound, in both Indian lore and the observations of European settlers, but in recent decades, rabies has been virtually unknown in wolf popula-tions.

In North America, there are few areas left where wolves are free from interference from human populations. In the wild, their pop-ulations may be able to increase rapidly if there is little interference such as hunting or trapping and there is an abundance of prey. One study of a protected area in Alaska indicated that a wolf population can increase by at least 20 percent per year, but only if it has not already established a maximum concentration. Natural controls on wolf populations other than hunting and trapping can include environmental influences, abundance of prey, and the presence of disease. Under natural conditions, wolf populations may fluctuate in size from year to year — often linked to the availability of food — but over time an average population size is maintained.

A long-running study of wolves on an isolated island in Lake Superior (Isle Royale National Park) has shown the relationship between predator and prey over time, with one population increasing or decreasing in response to the other. But if a wolf population is not confined to a limited geographic region such as an island, the influences are more complex and individuals or groups of wolves may leave an established hunting territory. It is estimated that there are now about 60,000 gray wolves and 300 red wolves in North America.

WOLF OR COYOTE?

"A black Wolfs Skin is worth a Beaver Skin among the Indians, being highly esteemed for helping old Aches, in old people, worn as a Coat; they are not man Kind [ed. note: would not attack humans] as in Ireland and other Countries, but do much harm by destroying of our English Cattle!" — Thomas Morton, 1637

Wolves in North America have had a long experience with mistaken identity. Large dogs, coyotes, and wolf-hybrids are often mistaken as wolves, even by some experienced naturalists. In the early era of settlement by Europeans, this problem was even more common than in modern times because there were a lot more wolves at the time, along with coyotes and dogs. In the western territories, the "wolf" label was frequently used indiscriminently to refer to coyotes, red wolves, and gray wolves, further compounding the identity problem.

In the modern era, increasing publicity about wolf reintroduction programs has resurrected this problem once again in some regions. In those areas where wolves have been re-released into the wild, reported sightings of wolves have increased, but studies have shown that most are actually of coyotes. In the northern United States, where most of the re-release programs are underway, the confusion may be greater because in the northern part of their natural range, coyotes are larger and often the size of small wolves.

HOW TO TELL THE DIFFERENCE BETWEEN A WOLF AND A COYOTE

WOLF   COYOTE

WOLF		COYOTE
larger	**BODY**	smaller
larger	**HEAD**	smaller
shorter, rounded	**EARS**	longer, pointed
broad, square	**MUZZLE**	narrow, pointed
larger	**TEETH**	smaller
longer	**LEGS**	shorter
larger than rear paws	**FRONT PAWS**	smaller than rear paws
smaller than front paws	**REAR PAWS**	larger than front paws
	FRONT PAW PRINT	

WOLF OR DOG?

"They be made much like a Mungrell, being big boned, lanky launched, deepe breasted, having a thicke necke, and head, pricke ears, and long snoute with dangerous teeth, long staring haire, and a great bush tail; it is thought of many that our English Mastiffes might be too hard for them; but it is no such matter, for they care no more for an ordinary Mastiffe, than an ordinary Mastiffe cares for a Curre ..."

— William A. Wood, 1635

Wolves are often mistaken for large dogs such as Huskies or Malamutes, and the reverse. Because many dogs may have been cross-bred with wolves, it may be impossible to tell the difference in some cases. In general, however, dogs have a wider chest. Dogs also usually hold their tails much lower than wolves and for almost all dog breeds — including cross-breeds — the tail tends to curl up.

Paw prints are another distinguishing difference between dogs and wolves. Wolf paw prints are almost always larger than even the largest dog prints. But the real difference is in the placement of the outside toes; in wolves, the toe pads and claw marks point forward. In dogs, the toe pads and claw marks are angled to the outside.

Another differing characteristic between the two animals is in their pattern of movement. In a normal gait, dogs bring their hind legs forward, stepping inside the track made by their front legs. In a wolf's gait, the hind leg moves forward in the same line as the front leg, placing its paw almost in the position left by the front paw.

WOLFING

"In early spring, when the cows begin to calve, the wolves sometimes wait upon the herds as they did of old on the buffalo, and snap up any calf that strays away from its mother. When hard pressed by hunger they will kill a steer or heifer, choosing the bitterest and coldest night to make the attack." — Theodore Roosevelt, 1885

Large-scale hunting and killing of wolves began in the mid-1800s. Wolves were sought because their pelts had value (although less than that of buffalo or other fur-bearing mammals such as beaver), they were thought to be a threat to humans (ranchers, farmers, gold miners), and they preyed on domesticated sheep, cattle, and pigs. During the 1870s, the rapid demise of the bison herds through hunting first led to widespread attacks by wolves on cattle and sheep. In most western states, bounties on wolves were first developed during this decade, leading to organized and systematic destruction of regional wolf populations. In Wyoming between 1883 and 1918, for instance, state records list 80,730 wolf bounties paid.

In Borden County, Texas, bounties in 1891 reflected the threat posed by various agricultural pests. Prairie dogs earned $3\frac{1}{2}$ cents, jackrabbits were worth $8\frac{1}{3}$ cents, bobcats got $1.00, and "coyote wolves" were $2.50. A dead wolf was pegged at $5.00. State-wide records show that between 1915 and 1936, supervised animal control programs accounted for 10,248 wolves. After 1936 and into the 1960s, predator eradication continued to target wolves, with 300 to 1,900 a year being killed.

In the eastern states, eradication programs began much earlier. Wolf bounties were common in many eastern states in the 1700s and in combination with the effects of an expanding rural population, logging, and clearing of land for agriculture, wolves were rare

As the number of buffalo declined on the western plains, buffalo bones and wolf hides attracted more traders.

by the middle of the 1800s. The last reported wolf in the wild in New York State was in 1897. Wolf bounties were established so early during the settlement period that they were an established and familiar value. Wolf skins thus became an accepted form of currency, tradable for goods or services except for the western regions, where there were no bounties and trade in other furs was a booming industry.

In 1630, the Massachusetts colony created the first wolf bounty in North America, enacted to reduce the loss of livestock. The Virginia colony had its own wolf bounty system in 1632. For every eight wolves, the bounty was one cow. Bounties were also often payable in tobacco, a common commodity at the time, but could also include other items. The bounties in the eastern colonies often

THE LEGAL WORD

Section 1. That whenever one-half of the legal voters of any county shall, by petition, ask the board of County Commissioners of such county to make an order allowing a bounty for wolf scalps, it shall be their duty to make such order: Provided, such bounty shall not exceed two dollars for each scalp.

Sec. 2. That whoever applies for the payment of said bounty, shall present to the board of County Commissioners, or to the County Clerk in vacation, the wolf's scalp including the ears of the wolf, and make affidavit that he killed the said wolf or wolves within the bounds of said county wherein the application is made.

Sec. 3. That whenever application is made, as set forth in section 2 of this act, it shall be the duty of the board of County Commissioners to cause an order to issue to the person thus applying, on the County Treasurer of said county, for the amount thus appropriated; and when such claim for bounty shall be allowed, it shall be the duty of the board of Commissioners to cause such scalps to be destroyed."

Approved, February 27, 1864.

— 1864, Session Laws of Kansas

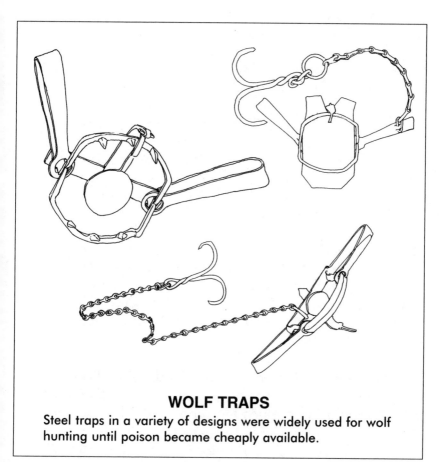

WOLF TRAPS
Steel traps in a variety of designs were widely used for wolf hunting until poison became cheaply available.

included other predators as well, such as bear, wildcats, foxes, and pumas.

In 1669, the English authorities in the Virginia colony commissioned a census of the local Indian population — members of the Powhatan tribe — in order to find out how many bowmen might be available to help in its wolf control program. Of about 2,900 Powhatans, 725 bowmen were listed as available. This plan to utilize Indian labor was rooted in a desire by the English colonists to find employment for the Indians in order to pacify them, as well as a need to reduce the wolves' predation. Unfortunately for the colonists, the Powhatans, like many tribes, had strong cultural beliefs about hunting and found it difficult to target wolves because they were not a traditional source of meat. Only a few Indians were recorded as redeeming wolf heads for bounty under this program, but white settlers did find it an attractive offer. So much so, in fact, that "poaching" of wolves beyond the boundaries of the colony became common. Following the failure to attract voluntary partic-ipation by the local Indians, the bounty legislation was amended to require an annual number of wolf heads from each Indian village and the authority for controlling the bounty program was passed to individual counties. In 1705, the bounty system was once again amended, this time requiring counties to pay higher bounties to Englishmen than Indians. Massachusetts, too, tried to use special incentives for the local Indian population to induce wolf hunting. Their bounty was amended in 1644 to offer Indians three quarts of

---

"Men haue bin forced to inuent and find out many deuices for the destroying of wolues, for the necessity hath taught them much learning, and it has become a shameful misery to indure the tyranny of such spoiling beastes without laboring for resistance and reuenge: for this cause they propounded also a reward to such as killed wolues for by the law of Dracho, he that killed a young wolfe received a tallent, and he that killed an old wolfe received two talents."

— E. Topsell, *The Historie of Four-Footed Beastes*, 1607

> "Motion made and carried that this association shall pay a reward of $5.00 for grown gray wolves, and $2.50 for cub wolves under 3 months old, killed upon the range of any member of this association after this date (Apr. 7, 1900), who is not in arrears of this association for any assessment. This money to be paid by the Treasurer, P.B. Scott. Upon a certificate to him issued by M.H. Murray, certifying that such wolves or cubs have been killed upon the range of some member of this association in good standing. And the fact of such killing of wolves or cubs shall be certified to Mr. M.H. Murray, by the owner of said range upon which the animals were killed."
>
> — *Book of Annual Meetings*
> Minutes of Bent-Prowers County Cattle
> and Horse Growers' Association (southern Colorado)

wine or three bushels of corn for every wolf head. However, widespread abuses of alcohol by colonists and Indians caused them to repeal this offer within a few years.

Bounty systems were set up by towns, counties, colonies, states, and independent groups such as cattlemen's associations. In some cases, more than one bounty might be paid for the same wolf. And throughout the history of the bounty system, more than one person actively engaged in fleecing the system, using dog and coyote ears, for example, to claim a reward for a wolf. Unscrupulous bounty seekers were also known to capture wolf pups and raise them to maturity before turning them in, a ploy that would gain them the higher reward often offered for adult animals.

In the pursuit of wolves, hunting was less common than wolf

baiting, because it was easier to kill more than one wolf with poison or traps than by shooting. In at least one instance, mange was deliberately planted in wolves in order to limit population growth with this disease. In the west, the most common method of killing wolves was with poison. Carcasses of cattle or bison were "salted" with crystals of strychnine or arsenic.

Traps were the most common method of killing wolves before the widespread use of poison began in the 1800s and their use dates back to the Middle Ages in Europe. The first traps were often pits, deep holes located along wolf runways. These pits were baited with meat or simply covered with brush. Some pits were equipped with sharpened stakes to impale the animals when they fell in. Eskimos

"The wolf, not merely figuratively, is at the door of many an Iowa farmer, but the real wolves, large wolves, prowl over the Iowa farms in increasing numbers, seeking what they may devour....Like the flea, when you put your hand on them they are not there. But their name is legion....Really it is a stain, a foul stigma, on the civilization and enterprise of the people of Iowa that these wolves remain and are frequently seen crossing the best cultivated farms, and even near the best towns in our State. What is the remedy, do you ask? Wipe out all trifling and unequal bounties and induce the legislature to provide a State bounty of $20 for the scalps of the old wolves and $5.00 for the young ones. The boys will then arm themselves with the best rifles of long range, will watch and hunt for the game, and speedily exterminate the lupine race."

— *Special Report of the Sheep Industry of the United States*
1892, Government Printing Office

"On the 5th of August [1868] at 10 o'clock PM a rabid wolf of the large grey species came into the post and charged round most furiously; he entered the hospital and attacked Corp. McGillicoddy C, C-3rd Inf. who was lying sick in the bed, biting him severely in the left hand & right arm. The left little finger was nearly taken off the wolf next dashed into a party of ladies and gentlemen sitting in the moonlight on Col. Wynkoop's porch and bit 1st Lieu. T. T. Thompson 3rd Inf. severely in both legs leaving there he soon after attacked and bit Priv. Thom. Mason C, of 10th Cav. member of the saber guard, lacerating his right foot severely and penetrating it in two places...He was a very large wolf and his long jaws and teeth presented a most formidable appearance. The wounds were thoroughly cauterized with nitrate of silver on the place...Sept. 1868. Corporal McGillicoddy C,C 3rd Inf. one of the men that were bitten by the rabid wolf on the 5th of August showed signs of commencing hydrophobia on the evening of the 6th inst. The symptoms were as usually described, were well marked and very characteristic he died on the morning of the 9th."

— Report of the Assistant Surgeon at
Fort Larned, Kansas, 1868

and other northern hunting cultures traditionally used piercers to kill wolves. A pierce was a sharpened flexible bone, usually taken from a whale, that was bent into a coil and frozen. Covered in animal fat or blubber, a wolf would usually swallow the object whole; in the wolf's stomach, body heat thawed the bone, which sprang into its original shape, fatally stabbing the wolf in the process.

Strychnine became the poison of choice for wolves — as well as other predators — in the mid-1800s. Although long available from seeds of a tree native to Australia and India (*Strychnos nux-vomica*), the drug was not manufactured in North America until 1834 and was widely available to traders and trappers in the West by the late 1840s. The first use of this commercial chemical was by wolfers, trappers in the western territories who specialized in wolf pelts. Poison was the method preferred by trappers because it left the skin in undamaged condition. What was an advantage for the wolfer, however, was a major threat to a wide range of wildlife in the wolf habitat. Other predators — including coyotes, red foxes, kit foxes, wolverines, ravens, eagles, hawks, magpies, skunks, and others — were killed indiscriminently along with the wolves, seriously disrupting the balance of nature throughout the western plains. In one historical record, a poisoned buffalo carcass on the plains of Kansas resulted in the deaths of 13 gray wolves, 15 coyotes, and about 40 skunks. Another reported buffalo poisoning in Kansas yielded 82 pelts, worth $2.50 each to the wolfer.

The wolf poison could cause even further damage because it remained active in the body wastes and saliva of the wolves it killed. Dying wolves salivated this poison onto grasses and the ground where it might later be ingested by horses, livestock, deer, or buffalo.

Wolfing was at its peak between 1860 and 1890, when the number of wolves increased and concentrated on the plains due to the tremendous number of buffalo carcasses left behind by buffalo hunters. The biggest market for wolf skins was the Russian army;

the pelts were used to make military overcoats. Wolfing was an occupation originally driven by the market for wolf skins, but in the latter part of the buffalo era in the western regions, local bounties from counties, states, and territories added an extra inducement. Bounties were commonly relied upon by ranch hands, drovers, and other settlers to earn extra income. The bounties were typically collected upon presentation of the ears of a wolf.

During the great boom in fur trapping beginning in the late 1700s, steel animal traps rapidly became the tool of choice for capturing wolves. The largest sizes were usually needed because of the strength of the animal. Wolves that freed themselves from such traps — often at the cost of a claw, toe, or part of the foot — became exceedingly wary of humans. Some of these animals may have also been inadvertently turned into livestock marauders, deprived of their traditional diet because of lameness.

Set-guns were also used to kill wolves. These devices were usually shotguns, wired to a piece of bait. When the bait was grabbed by a wolf, the gun discharged. Another widespread practice by wolfers was den hunting, searching for dens containing litters of young wolf puppies. The puppies were either killed or captured and raised to full size, when they were killed for their pelts or the local bounty.

Wolf hunting was a passive activity when traps or poison were used, but a more active form was also popular, hunting with horses and dogs. As early as the mid-1800s, dog breeds from Europe were imported just to hunt wolves. Irish wolfhounds and Russian borzois were specially bred to be able to outrun wolves, but other breeds were also commonly employed in this practice, including greyhounds and a variety of types originally bred to hunt deer.

Wolf hunts were sometimes pursued as a form of sport, with organizations or informal groups of citizens involved. Occasionally, grandiose hunting spectacles were mounted, involving hundreds of people, dogs, and horses. These were known as wolf drives and sometimes referred to as circle hunts. The drives were arranged to move the animals into a centralized clearing where clubs and gunfire were used to dispatch them. In the early history of Rhode Island, wolf drives were reported more than once as early as the mid-1600s. Wolf drives were still being held in the late 1800s in some western states.

PET WOLVES

"He's mad that trusts in the tameness of a wolf, a horse's health, a boy's love, or a whore's oath."

— William Shakespeare (*King Lear*)

Throughout North America, some Indian tribes were known to occasionally capture wolf puppies and raise them as pets. Though domesticated, these animals were different from the domestic dog that was widely dispersed through the continent. At times, dog and wolf have naturally interbred and produced hybrid offspring. Eastern Indian tribes who kept both dogs and hybrid wolves used different names for the two types of animals. The Mohicans called their wolf-dogs the anun-neen-dee-a-oo, or "original dog."

According to some observations and records, both tamed wolves and wolf-hybrids were sometimes used in place of dogs for some tasks. These included pulling sleds and carrying loads. In the modern era, however, the wolf has attracted the attention of animal lovers less for practical purposes than for companionship and the pride of ownership. So many people now desire these breeds that a thriving market exists for these puppies in many parts of the country. Unfortunately, because of the very traits that characterize wolves, ownership does not come without hazard. The number of incidents of attacks and deaths from captive wolves and wolf-hybrids is on the rise and has already forced the adoption of new rules about their presence in some municipalities, counties, and states.

In general, animal protection organizations and wolf behavior experts find nothing but negatives for this kind of interaction. In captivity, the wolf traits produce an animal that requires more space, isolation, and special handling than the average dog owner is capable of providing. Dogs have been bred for thousands of generations to produce animals that coexist naturally with humans as part of their social structure; in effect, they are canines who cooperate with humans as if they were part of the human family. Wolves raised among humans don't act human, but expect their human companions to act like wolves.

The result is often confrontations between wolf and owners, aggressiveness, and attacks. The tragedy of this trend in pet ownership is human misery as well as a diminished life experience for the animal. Between 1979 and 1994, twelve deaths were reported from attacks by these pets.

One offshoot of the expanding number of wolf-hybrids and adopted wolves is the creation of sanctuaries to provide homes for animals that have outgrown their welcome among humans. Because they do not have the necessary experience to survive in the wild — and lack the necessary natural shyness to avoid human contact — these sanctuaries in some cases may be the only alternative to euthanasia.

REINTRODUCTION

"Owing to the openness and natural advantages for hunters in that region [Colorado and Wyoming], all big game animals are disappearing faster than they ever did in any of our eastern forests, but what of the wolf? ... With four practical ways open for his undoing in the West, he not only grows more abundant, but adds new territory to his possessions and refuses to be 'outed,' while all other of the larger animals of the West are rapidly disappearing."

— Emerson Carney, 1902

Few wildlife programs have resulted in as much controversy and emotion as the effort to reintroduce wolves back into parts of their traditional range. Both gray wolf and red wolf reintroduction programs have been underway since the 1980s, with varying degrees of success. Reintroduction as it is now being pursued involves a variety of political, ecological, and agricultural issues, many of them in conflict with one another.

The most volatile issue arising from reintroduction is the potential for the newly-arrived wolves to prey upon already established livestock within striking distance of their intended range. Although no ultimate solutions are yet available, short-term answers include controlled trapping or killing of individual wolves if and when they resort to livestock as a food source. Following the recent introduction of a wolf pack into Yellowstone Park, this type of predation has already occurred. Other problems include wolf deaths from motor vehicles, harassment by poachers, and interference with their natural lifestyle caused by park visitors.

Following reintroduction, wolves quickly begin altering the existing balance of nature in their new habitats. Populations of herd animals that have roamed freely for generations without the pressure of wolf predation are the first to be affected. The Yellowstone reintroduction program has also demonstrated other changes in the ecosystem, including a rapid and severe impact on the resident population of coyotes, a natural competitor of wolves and present in large numbers because of the wolve's absence. With the return of wolves, the coyotes have initially found a bountiful new source of food in the carcasses of herd animals killed by the larger predators. But wolves instinctively feel threatened by coyotes, and the Yellowstone packs have been observed killing large numbers of their smaller rivals. Although this is only one stage in the process of reintroduction, eventually the wolves, coyotes, and their prey will achieve a natural balance more typical of the habitat before it was disrupted by European settlement.

REINTRODUCTION PROGRAMS

RED WOLF

- Alligator River National Wildlife Refuge
  northeastern North Carolina
- Bulls Island, Cape Romai National Wildlife Refuge
  South Carolina
- Horn Island, Gulf Islands National Seashore
  Mississippi
- St. Vincent National Wildlife Refuge
  Florida
- Great Smoky Mountains National Park
  North Carolina, Tennessee

GRAY WOLF

- Yellowstone National Park
  Montana
- U.S. Forest Service
  central Idaho

PROFILE OF AN EXTINCT ANIMAL?

"Now the hungry lion roars,
And the wolf behowls the moon ..."
— William Shakespeare (*Much Ado About Nothing*)

The Mexican wolf (*Canis lupus baileyi*), a subspecies of the gray wolf, is one North American wolf that it is too late to save in the wild. Before the arrival of European settlers, the Mexican wolf ranged from central Mexico northward through most of Arizona, New Mexico, and Texas, feeding primarily on the Coues white-tailed deer. Wolf eradication programs were enacted within this territory as early as the mid-1800s, with the result that by the early 1900s, few wolves remained throughout much of their original range.

A few wolves remained north of the border until the 1970s, when the last animals were trapped, poisoned, or shot. In 1976, this subspecies was officially placed on the endangered species list, and a few animals were captured for breeding in recovery programs. No evidence has been found since the late 1980s that any Mexican wolves remain in the wild, but more than 100 survive in zoos and wildlife centers in the United States and Mexico. Biologists hope to begin a release of some of these survivors back into the wild in selected areas before the end of the century, although attempts mounted so far have been thwarted by opposition from ranchers and local politics.

RESORCES

O rganizations that deal with animal and wildlife issues can provide additional information about squirrels, as well as being
useful in local, regional, or national efforts to protect natural habitats and endangered species.

INTERNATIONAL WILDLIFE INFORMATION

World Conservation Monitoring Centre
219 Huntingdon Road   Cambridge CB30DL United Kingdom
44-0-1223-277314

NORTH AMERICAN WILDLIFE INFORMATION

National Audubon Society
700 Broadway, New York, NY 10003
212-979-3000

Wildlife Society
5410 Grosvenor Lane
Bethesda, MD 20814-2197
301-897-9770

The Nature Conservancy
1815 N. Lynn Street
Arlington, VA 22209
703-841-5300

Wilderness Society
900 17th Street NW
Washington, DC 20006-2596
202-833-2300

Friends of the Earth
1025 Vermont Ave. NW 3rd Floor
Washington, DC 20005
202-783-7400

WOLF ORGANIZATIONS

Friends of the Wolf
P.O. Box 21032, Glebe Postal Outlet
Ottawa, Ontario K1S 5N1 Canada

International Wolf Center
1369 Highway 169
Ely, MN 55731-8129

Mission: Wolf
P.O. Box 211, Silver Cliff, CO 81249
719-746-2919

Red Wolf Newsletter
The Zoo Society/Point Defiance
Zoo and Aquarium
5400 N. Pearl St, Tacoma, WA 98407

Timber Wolf Alliance
Northland College
Ashland, WI 54806-3999

Timber Wolf Preservation Society
6669 S. 76th Street
Greendale, WI 53129

Wolf Education and Resource Center
P.O. Box 3832, Ketchum, ID 83340

Wolf Haven
3111 Offut Lake Road
Tenino, WA 98589

Wolf Hollow
Route 133, Ipswich, MA 09138

Wolf Park
Battle Ground, IN 47920

Wolf Sanctuary
P.O. Box 760, Eureka, MO 63025

The Wolf Sanctuary Review
P.O. Box 760, Eureka, MO 63025
314-938-5900

Wolf Society of Great Britain
Prospect House, Charlton
Kilmersdon, Bath BA3 5TN

ONLINE RESOURCES

Computer connections to information can prove useful to those interested in wildlife and nature. Online resources include reference material, discussions with like-minded individuals, communications with agencies and organizations involved with wildlife, and access to up-to-date information and schedules. As the online industry is growing and evolving rapidly, listed resources may change and new resource may pop up unexpectedly. To search for additional resources, look for menu listings or search for topics associated with **wildlife, wild animals, nature, ecology,** and **environmental resources**. Also look for topics listed by the common name of an animal, such as **wolf** or **wolves**.

Many libraries now provide access to their materials through online connections. Using terminals inside libraries — or dialing in from a remote location — use the same search strategies to locate books, reference material, and periodicals.

AMERICA ONLINE

Go to <Nature Conservancy> or <Network Earth Online>

COMPUSERVE

Go to <Earth Forum>, <The Great Outdoors Forum>, <Outdoor Network>, or <Animal Forum: Wildlife/Rehab>

WORLD WIDE WEB

Environmental Communicator <www.nwf.org/nwf/home.html>

Friends of the Wolf <www.carleton.ca/~whipwell/wolf.html>

International Wolf Center <www.wolf.org>

Mission: Wolf <www.puzzlegulch.com/Mission:Wolf>

National Audubon Society <www.audubon.org/audubon>

Red wolf information <www.fws.gov/bio-rwol.html>

Sierra Club <www.sierraclub.org>

U.S. Fish & Wildlife Service <www.fws.gov>

The Wildlife Society <www.us.net/wildlife>

Wolf Haven <members.aol.com/wolf4haven/haven1.htm>

Wolf Park <tigerden.com/Wolf-park/Welcome.html>

World Conservation Conitoring Centre <www.wcmc.org.uk>

BIBLIOGRAPHY

Audubon, John James, and Bachman, John. *The Quadrupeds of North America*. 1851, 1854, V.G. Audubon (New York, NY).

Baring-Gould, Sabine. *The Book of Werewolves*. 1865, Smith, Elder & Company (London, England). Republished 1995, Senate (London, England).

Bauer, Erwin A. *Wild Dogs: The Wolves, Coyotes and Foxes of North America*. 1994, Chronicle Books.

Botkin, Danile B. *Our Natural History: The Lessons of Lewis and Clark*. 1995, Grosset/Putnam.

Bourliere, Francois. *The Natural History of Mammals*. 1954, Alfred A. Knopf.

Buffon, Georges. *Buffon's Natural History of Man, the Globe, and of Quadrapeds*. 1879, Hurst & Company (New York, NY). Translated from the French.

Burbank, James C. *Vanishing Lobo: The Mexican Wolf and the Southwest*. 1990, Johnson Books (Boulder, CO).

Burt, William Henry. *A Field Guide to the Mammals: North America North of Mexico* (3rd edition). 1980, Houghton Mifflin Company.

Busch, Robert H. *The Wolf Almanac: A Celebration of Wolves and Their World*. 1995, Lyons and Burford.

Caras, Roger A. *Dangerous to Man: Wild Animals, A Definitive Study of Their Reputed Dangers to Man*. 1964, Chilton Books.

Crandall, Lee S. *The Management of Wild Mammals in Captivity*. 1964, University of Chicago Press.

Dale-Green, Patricia. *Lore of the Dog*. 1967, Houghton Mifflin Company.

Dary, David A. *The Buffalo Book: The Full Saga of the American Animal*. 1974, 1989. Swallow Press/Ohio University Press.

de Gubernatis, Angelo. *Zoological Mythology*. 1872, Trubner & Company (London, England). Republished: 1968, Singing Tree Press (Detroit, MI).

Dinsmore, James. *A Country So Full of Game: The Story of Wildlife in Iowa*. 1994, University of Iowa Press (Iowa City, IA).

Duden, Gottfried. *Report on a Journey to the Western States of North America*. 1980, State Historical Society/University of Missouri Press (Columbia, MO).

Fischer, Hank. *Wolf Wars: The Remarkable Inside Story of the Restoration of Wolves to Yellowstone*. 1995, Falcon Press (Helena, MT).

Fleharty, Eugene D. *Wild Animals and Settlers on the Great Plains*. 1995, University of Oklahoma Press (Norman, OK).

Fox, M.W., ed. *The Wild Canids: Their Systematics, Behavioral Ecology and Evolution.* 1975, Van Nostrand Reinhold.

Garfield, Viola E. and Forrest, Linn A. *The Wolf and the Raven: Totem Poles of Southeastern Alaska.* 1948, University of Washington Press (Seattle, WA).

Haines, Frances. *The Buffalo.* 1970, 1995, University of Oklahoma Press (Norman, OK).

Halfpenny, James. *A Field Guide to Mammal Tracking in Western America.* 1986, Johnson Books (Boulder, CO).

Hall, E. Raymond. *The Mammals of North America* (second edition) 1981, John Wiley & Sons Inc.

Harrington, Fred H. and Paquet, Paul C., eds. *Wolves of the World: Perspectives of Behavior, Ecology, and Conservation.* 1982, Noyes Publications (Park Ridge, NJ).

Herrick. C.L. *Mammals of Minnesota.* 1892, Geological and Natural History Survey of Minnesota.

Hughes, J. Donald. *American Indian Ecology.* 1983, Texas Western Press (El Paso, TX).

Lempfert, O.C. *Paw Prints: How to Identify Rare and Common Mammals by Their Tracks.* 1972, Exposition Press (Jericho, NY).

Link, Mike and Crowley, Kate. *Following the Pack: The World of Wolf Research.* 1994, Voyageur Press Inc. (Stillwater, MN).

Lopez, Barry Holston. *Of Wolves and Men.* 1978, Charles Scribner's Sons.

Matthiessen, Peter. *Wildlife in America.* 1959, 1987, Penguin Books.

Mead, James R. *Hunting and Trading on the Great Plains, 1859–1875.* 1986, University of Oklahoma Press (Norman, OK).

Mech, L. David. *The Wolf: The Ecology and Behavior of an Endangered Species.* 1970, The Natural History Press (Garden City, NY).

Mills, Enos A. *Wild Life in the Rockies.* 1909, Houghton Mifflin Company (reissued in 1988, University of Nebraska Press).

Murie, Olaus J. *A Field Guide to Animal Tracks: The Peterson Field Guide Series.* 1975, Houghton Mifflin Company.

Nelson, Edward W. *Wild Animals of North America.* 1918, National Geographic Society.

Norman, Howard. *Northern Tales: Traditional Stories of Eskimo and Indian Peoples.* 1990, Pantheon Books (New York, NY).

Nowak, Ronald M. *Walker's Mammals of the World* (5th Edition). 1991, Johns Hopkins University Press (Baltimore, MD).

Olsen, Stanley J. *Origins of the Domestic Dog: The Fossil Record.* 1985, University of Arizona Press (Tucson, AZ).

Otten, Charlotte F., ed. *A Lycanthropy Reader: Werewolves in Western Culture.* 1986, Syracuse University Press (Syracuse, NY).

Porter, J. Hampden. *Wild Beasts: A Study of the Characters and Habits of the Elephant, Lion, Leopard, Panther, Jaguar, Tiger, Puma, Wolf, and Grizzly Bear.* 1894, Charles Scribner's Sons.

Porter, J.R. and Russell, W.M.S. *Animals in Folklore.* 1978, Rowman & Littlefield (Totowa, NJ).

Rand, A.L. *Mammals of the Eastern Rockies and Western Plains of Canada.* 1948, Canada Department of Mines and Resources.

Rountree, Helen C. *Pocahontas's People: The Powhattan Indians of Virginia Through Four Centuries.* 1990. University of Oklahoma Press (Norman, OK).

Rowland, Beryl. *Animals with Human Faces: A Guide to Animal Symbolism.* 1973, University of Tennessee Press.

Rue, Leonard Lee III. *Wolves: A Portrait of the Animal World.* 1993, Magma Books (Leicester, England).

Rutter, Russell J. and Pimlott, Douglas H. *The World of the Wolf.* 1968, J.B. Lippincott Company.

Seton, Ernest Thompson. *Great Historic Animals: Mainly About Wolves.* 1937, Charles Scribner's Sons.

Steinhart, Peter. *The Company of Wolves.* 1995, Alfred A. Knopf.

Taylor, Robert J. *Predation.* 1984, Chapman & Hall Ltd. (London, England).

Thiel, Richard P. *The Timber Wolf in Wisconsin: The Death and Life of a Majestic Predator.* 1993, University of Wisconsin Press.

Van Gelder, Richard G. *Mammals of the National Parks.* 1982, Johns Hopkins University Press (Baltimore, MD).

Walker, James R. *Lakota Belief and Ritual.* 1980, 1991, University of Nebraska Press.

Whitaker, John O. Jr. *National Audubon Society Field Guide to North American Mammals.* 1980, Alfred A. Knopf.

Wiley, Farida A., ed. *Ernest Thompson Seton's America.* 1954, Devin-Adair Company (New York, NY).

Wolves in American Culture Committee. *Wolf!* 1986, Northword Inc. (Ashland, WI).

Wootton, Anthony. *Animal Folklore, Myth and Legend.* 1986, Blandford Press (Dorset, England).

Young, Stanley P. and Goldman, Edward A. *The Wolves of North America.* 1944, The American Wildlife Institute (Washington, DC).

Young, Stanley Paul. *The Wolf in North American History.* 1946, Caxton Printers, Ltd. (Caldwell, ID).

INDEX

Other Titles of Interest from Johnson Books

Johnson Nature Series

Squirrels: A Wildlife Handbook
Kim Long

A Field Guide to Mammal Tracking in North America
James Halfpenny

Winter: An Ecological Handbook
James Halfpenny and Roy Ozanne

Soul Among Lions: The Cougar as Peaceful Adversary
Harley Shaw

From Grassland to Glacier:
The Natural History of Colorado and the Surrounding Region
Revised Edition
Cornelia Fleischer Mutel and John C. Emerick

Island in the Plains: A Black Hills Natural History
Edward Raventon

Pocket Nature Guides

Millie Miller and Cyndi Nelson

Desert Critters: Plants and Animals of the Southwest
Hummers: Hummingbirds of North America
Talons: North American Birds of Prey
Early Bird: Western Backyard Birds
Early Bird: Eastern Backyard Birds
Painted Ladies: Butterflies of North America
Chanterelle: A Rocky Mountain Mushroom Book
Kinnikinnick: Rocky Mountain Flowers
Sierra: Sierra Mountain Flowers